P9-EED-803

Our Independence and the Constitution

On July 4, 1776, the citizens of Philadelphia gathered to hear the first reading of the Declaration of Independence. At the end of the stirring speech, the people shouted and roared, and all the bells in Philadelphia—including the famous Liberty Bell— rang and rang.

But declaring independence from England was just the first of the new nation's problems. In *Our Independence and the Constitution,* Dorothy Canfield Fisher creates a lively picture of those early days of freedom when George Washington, Ben Franklin, James Madison, and other American leaders worked passionately to hammer out a constitution that would hold the new country together and, at the same time, be satisfactory to each of the thirteen states.

The fact that we have celebrated the 200th anniversary of the signing of the Constitution of the United States proves that those wise American statesmen succeeded beyond their wildest dreams.

Our
Independence
and the
Constitution

Dorothy Canfield Fisher

RANDOM HOUSE • NEW YORK

Copyright 1950 by Dorothy Canfield Fisher. Copyright renewed 1978 by
Sarah J. Scott. All rights reserved under International and Pan-American
Copyright Conventions. Published in the United States by Random House,
Inc., New York, and simultaneously in Canada by Random House of
Canada Limited, Toronto.

Library of Congress Cataloging-in-Publication Data:
Fisher, Dorothy Canfield, 1879–1958. Our independence and the
constitution.
   (Landmark books) Reprint. Originally published: New York : Random
House, 1950. SUMMARY: Portrays the writing of the Declaration of Inde-
pendence and the formation of the Constitution through the eyes of one
Philadelphia family. 1. United States. Declaration of Independence—Juve-
nile literature. 2. United States—Constitution—Juvenile literature. 3.
United States—Constitutional history—Juvenile literature. 4. United
States—Politics and government—Revolution, 1775–1783—Juvenile litera-
ture. [1. United States. Declaration of Independence. 2. United States—
Constitutional history. 3. United States—Politics and government—Revolu-
tion, 1775–1783] I. Title.   E221.F57   1987   973.3'13   87-4656
ISBN: 0-394-89175-9 (trade); 0-394-90305-6 (lib. bdg.)

Manufactured in the United States of America
1   2   3   4   5   6   7   8   9   0

Contents

Part I

Part II

Our
Independence
and the
Constitution

Part I

Philadelphia
1776

1

Philadelphia's Welcome

The First Continental Congress had sent a polite letter begging King George not to listen to bad advisers but to give his loyal and faithful American subjects the general rights of all free British subjects. Also those rights specially granted in their charters. To show that they meant business, the members of the First Continental Congress had said they would wait a fair time for a ship to cross the Atlantic with their petition and to come back with the answer. If the British government did not promise to do what they asked, the members agreed that the next step was for the American colonies not to buy anything from England or sell anything to England. That idea had worked, almost ten years before, with the Stamp Act. British merchants who did a very profitable business with the Americans had lost a lot of money when the colonies stopped trading with them. They protested loudly. The Stamp Act was repealed. The Americans hoped it would work again.

Then, in October 1774, the delegates to that first Congress had gone home.

Now, six months later, on May 10th, 1775, they were coming back to Philadelphia to take part in another Continental Congress. But this second one was going to be very different and much more important.

Only three weeks before that date Paul Revere had galloped at night from Boston shouting his warning, "The Regulars are out!" By dawn on April 19th, red-coated British soldiers at Lexington had fired on the American Militia. By ten o'clock in the morning, British soldiers had fallen back from American troops at the North Bridge in Concord. By dark that night, the British forces had retreated on the run to Boston, chased by Massachusetts sharp-shooting Minute Men.

For years Americans and British had been arguing and disputing, more and more angrily, about whether American colonies should take orders from the English king and his ministers and friends without any say-so of their own about what the orders should be. It had been like water in a kettle on a hot stove, first simmering, then boiling, then sending off a long stream of scalding steam from the spout. With the news of the actual fighting at Concord, the kettle cover had finally blown off with a tremendous bang.

Ordinary Massachusetts men in their everyday work clothes, snatching up their muskets as they raced out of their homes, had not run away scared from the terrible British Regulars, but had stood up and fought—and won. For years the English king and his friends had said over and over that the colonists were cowards. Maybe they had enough spunk to fight Indians, but the Americans would "run like rabbits," so the London newspapers kept saying, if they ever saw real British soldiers in battle line marching against them.

Now all America knew better. As the news from Lexington went racing through the colonies like wildfire, people cheered and shouted in relief and joy. And because they now knew that trained army soldiers and officers are not always better fighters than citizens, they saw the door to their future swing open.

All America rejoiced—those who wanted to go on being English subjects just as much as those who wanted to be independent of England. For, that spring of 1775 when the news from Lexington and Concord came in, there were plenty of colonists who wanted to remain English. But they threw their hats into the air and cheered just as loudly as anybody else over the news that ordinary colonists really had fought against English troops. What they wanted was to be subjects of the English king, but also to have the king run the government by English law.

But the man who was king in England wanted to act

as kings did in France or Prussia—which was any way they felt like acting. He didn't actually break any laws. The English Constitution stood up in front of him like a fence. But most fences have holes in them. The king was getting through the holes. He still went through the motions of doing the legal thing—such as having a Cabinet of Ministers, made up of rich, well-known English lords whose advice he was supposed to take. He took their advice, all right, as long as they advised him to do what he already wanted to do. But if any member of his Cabinet didn't say yes to his every idea, the king saw to it that he lost his job as minister. He not only dismissed him, he made life miserable for him afterward—for him, and for his whole family when that was possible.

Americans, however, had been saying no to the king. It was harder for him to make life miserable for Americans. For one thing they were too far away from London. And for another, most of them earned their own living by doing something useful. They didn't, like many of the English lords and their families, depend on the king for soft jobs with big salaries and little work. The king had grown more and more angry with the Massachusetts folks, who kept saying no to him, and had ended by sending to Boston ten thousand regular British soldiers. If the Massachusetts people wouldn't say yes of their own accord, he would make them. And if he could make Massachusetts people give in to him, he could do the same thing to the other colonies any time he took a notion to. This meant that if he could and if he did, the people in the American colonies would be like prisoners in a jail. They would have to do what the armed guards told them to, no matter what.

So if you had been an American in 1775—whether you were one of those who wanted to cut loose from England altogether, or one of those who loved the best of English ideas and ways and wanted to go on living under English law—you too would have jumped up from your chair at the news from Lexington and Concord and shouted for joy.

Philadelphia people usually took things quietly. They didn't take the news of the fighting at Lexington and Concord quietly. Their hearts were bursting with feelings too big for words. But there are other ways than words, often better ways, to say what is burning in your heart. That May in 1775, a month after the fight at the bridge in Concord, Philadelphia found a way to give a tremendous shout of pride and hope and courage, without speaking a single word.

This is what they did. The first delegates to that important second Congress were due on May 9. Philadelphia, in 1775, was the biggest city in America, twice as big as Boston; but by the day after the news had come in that it had been British, not Americans, who had "run like rabbits" on the retreat from Lexington to Boston, there was scarcely a single one of all the thirty thousand people in the city who did not know that on May 9th their town was going to give those delegates a welcome nobody would ever forget.

The morning of the 9th, out on the road where the travelers were to come in, several hundred armed men on horseback stood waiting, their band in front of them. They had sent lookouts farther along the road to catch the first glimpse of the approaching delegates and gallop back at top speed to say they were coming. The mounted men on their fine, shiny-coated horses stood ready in taut, straight ranks stretching a long way down the country road. The band players in front, also on horseback, fingered the keys of their trumpets, blew softly into their flutes and fifes to be sure they were in tune, held their drumsticks poised over the tightly stretched drumheads. The horses tossed their heads, their well-oiled hoofs glittering as they shifted their feet nervously. They knew beforehand how loud that band was going to sound when it broke loose.

Ahead of them the pleasant, tree-shaded earth of the country road stretched empty and waiting. They were all straining their eyes to see the messenger hurrying back. Before there was anything to see, the bandmaster's sharp ears caught the rapid pulse of a gallop. *"All ready!"* he shouted warningly to the band.

The bandmaster brought down his arm. The band burst out into that thundering crash of brass and drums which the horses had known would come, but which all the same was so loud that they flung up their heads, their manes tossing wildly.

"Forward MARCH!" cried the officer in command.

They stepped off to the blaring music of the band. At the turn of the road, ahead, a little group of travelers on horseback came into sight.

They drew rein, surprised, and sat their horses in the road a little uncertainly. But they had no reason to be uncertain. Everything to the last step had been planned out beforehand.

Just before the noisy band reached them, the command "Halt!" was given. On a one-*two* beat all the marchers stopped at the same instant.

"Present AR-R-RMS!" sang out the officer in command. The swords flashed out. Holding to this salute of honor, the band and the first half of the company swung their horses about to the command of "About FACE!"

The other half of the company divided into two lines and drew their horses to each side of the road. The band, tootling and braying proudly, their horses stepping high, passed between these lines. The first detachment of the company marched after them. Then those who made up the side lines, their bare swords still held in the salute of honor, moved forward, went past the travelers on horseback, and wheeled to the center of the road behind the men they were welcoming.

The maneuver was over. An advance guard of honor now marched in front of the delegates, and a rear guard of honor behind them. The travelers sat up straighter in their saddles, pulled the skirts of their riding coats down more smoothly, and felt of their cocked hats to be sure they were straight on their heads. Then they urged their horses forward, trying to look as though they were used to being met by hundreds of mounted men and a band every time they took a ride.

But that was not all. They had not gone very far before they saw, looking down the road past their mounted advance guard and band, long lines of soldiers on foot. They too were standing at attention, presenting arms. They too had a band of their own banging away for dear life, not to be outdone by the troops on horseback.

The same maneuver was carried out as with the mounted welcomers. The foot soldiers divided and again fell into line at the head and at the rear of the company. Their band now marched at the end, and the procession was so very long that their music didn't interfere with the mounted band bang-whanging away at the front.

In the middle rode the delegates. By the time they reached Philadelphia, there were more people looking at them than some of them had ever seen together in all their lives.

All the delegates came from smaller cities, some from the country, where a few hundred people were considered a real crowd. On that May 9th, 1775, at least half the population of Philadelphia was out on the streets to welcome them. Fifteen thousand people dressed in their best clothes stood crowded together, bursting into cheers,

"Hurrah! Hurrah!" when the little group of riders came along in the middle of the guard of honor.

Now the bells began! Above the loud hurrah!-hurrahs! which half drowned out the two brass bands, every steeple of every church in the city began to clang joyfully.

The horses stepped proudly, the drawn swords of the riders glittered, the infantry swung forward in time to the whirling music of whichever band was nearest to them. The crowds in the streets grew thicker and thicker, they cheered more and more loudly, their hearts beating faster in the uproar. After a while the shouts were not only "Hurrah! Hip-hip-hip-hurrah!" but *"Lexington! Lexington! Concord!"*

By this time, the delegates being welcomed into the Second Continental Congress were as excited as everybody else. Their faces were flushed, their eyes were shining. They were a part of all this. Everybody there was a part. And the whole was something bigger than any of them had ever dreamed of. The women in the crowds lining the streets waved their handkerchiefs. The men waved their hats. They all cheered and cheered, their feelings far beyond what could have been put into words.

The procession wound on and on through the crowded streets and finally turned into Chestnut Street. Before the fine Pennsylvania State House (now called Constitution Hall), they drew up in a formation which left a broad lane open for the delegates to the front door of the big brick building.

Men sprang forward to hold the horses. The delegates dismounted, walked forward, and mounted the steps. As they did, the noise rose to a hurricane, the church bells flinging down their loud, brazen sound waves, the drumsticks rolling furiously on the drums, the trumpets and the shouts rising to the clouds.

The delegates turned on the top steps, took off their hats, bowed to the crowds. The doors opened. They walked in. The doors closed behind them.

The welcome was over. The horsemen and foot soldiers did an about-face and marched away. The crowds of men and women and children hung around for a while getting their breath, looking up at the closed doors and windows behind which the meetings of the Second Continental Congress were to be held. Then they too drifted away to their own homes, to live it all over again in talk.

The street outside was empty, except for the men holding the horses of the delegates, a wandering cat or two, and some small children who chalked out a hopscotch game and began to hop around its squares.

Inside the Assembly Hall, cool and quiet after the streets, the delegates stood wiping the sweat from their foreheads and necks, or dropped into chairs to get their breath. They knew that they were there for very serious business. Some of them were rather pale. Those who had sat down took off their hats and held them on their knees.

"A warm welcome, sir," said one to a man near him. The other nodded. "Yes, very fine. Very fine," he agreed. "I had no idea that the people here felt so united on this question. Do they in your province?" he asked.

A third delegate spoke quickly. "I wish everyone in my province of Delaware could have heard those cheers. But I shall write back about this. They must know."

Two men walking past this group stopped. One of them said, "Was that not a noble welcome!"

"Very fine," said the other. "All the same—all the same—" He paused.

There was a silence. Then a tall, ruddy-faced man called across the room, "You mean, I take it, that although the welcome was joyful, what is before us here is not joyful, but the hardest kind of hard work."

There was another silence. Then the first man said, "Well, no, Colonel Washington, I wasn't thinking of hard work. Rather that things have now gone beyond loyal petitions to the king. We've other things to do, and—fine welcome or not—we may, every one of us, be hanged for our part in this—if we don't succeed."

This time there was no silence. Several men spoke at once, quickly, all in the same words. "But we *will* succeed," they said.

2

Collecting Delegates

There had been plenty of boys and girls among the thousands of Philadelphia folks who had stood cheering and shouting when the delegates to the Congress arrived. And there were plenty of youngsters among the crowds who, for months afterward, walked slowly as they passed the State House, or stood in front of it in silent groups, watching the delegates arriving for a morning session or leaving when the afternoon session was over. Everybody knew how important the Congress was to America. Everybody was anxious—some people were even frightened—about what was going to happen. Little else was talked about in Philadelphia.

Naturally the children felt this too—especially the older ones, who realized from the tone of the grownups' voices that something serious and not-to-be-forgotten was going on at the meetings. They listened to as much of their elders' talk as they could hear. They asked their parents questions when they didn't understand. They looked hard, as their fathers and mothers did, at the men from other colonies, delegates to the Congress, whenever a glimpse was to be had of them.

If it was near time for a session to end, the youngsters hung around in front of the State House waiting for the big doors to open and the delegates to come out, to go back to the boardinghouses or hotels where they were staying.

The delegates usually looked tired. Sometimes they looked glum and downcast. Sometimes they seemed excited. Sometimes they were just serious, and walked slowly in little groups. Their faces, often troubled, often anxious, sometimes pale, sometimes deeply flushed, turned toward each other as they talked.

The Philadelphia children watched those delegates to the Continental Congress coming and going to the State House for more than a year before anything very exciting happened again. For long months Philadelphia streets were quiet. The older boys and girls came to distinguish delegates from other men because their clothes somehow didn't look just like those of Philadelphia people, and because they were nearly always so serious-looking.

Everybody soon came to know Dr. Benjamin Franklin because he was so old, and Mr. Thomas Jefferson because he looked so young. And Mr. John Hancock, President of the Congress. They knew John Hancock from the style he put on. Such style! It was as good as a show to see that great coach of his go by. He was inside it somewhere, of course, but all they saw of him was a flash of expensive clothes through the window. With him were his four servants, tricked out in fancy uniforms like dressed-up monkeys and mounted on splendid horses with gleaming saddles and bridles. And before *and* behind that great carriage clattered a guard of *fifty* men on horseback, each one with a sword, not pushed down into its leather case but bared and flashing in the light.

"Whatever in the world makes Mr. Hancock do so much show-off business?" people would ask each other, and someone would always answer, "Oh, the Hancocks were poor folks till his uncle's time. He wants to be sure everybody knows they have money now."

The Philadelphia children soon had him on their list of Congress members whom they recognized on the street, along with Dr. Franklin. Nobody who had seen that old man could ever forget him. Especially if they had had the good luck to see Dr. Franklin smile. There was something like sunshine about his smile and the way his keen old eyes softened. People spoke about that as much as about his being so celebrated, the most famous American alive. Evidently Mr. Jefferson from Virginia liked the old philosopher, too, for they were often together. The children who lived near Dr. Franklin's house sometimes watched as the simple little carriage carried the stout old man to the State House. But on fair days, when it was neither too hot nor too cold, they saw the old doctor

18

trudge home on foot, leaning on young Mr. Jefferson's arm.

Once, a small girl who lived on Dr. Franklin's street looked up from the sandpile where she was playing and saw that the short, broad, stooped old doctor and the slim, tall young delegate had stopped beside her. Smiling pleasantly, Mr. Jefferson leaned down to pat her head. "I have a little daughter at home, just about your size," he said. "She has hair just the color of yours. Her name's Patsy. What's yours?"

"Debby," said the child, not much interested. People were always saying they had little girls at home "just your size."

But after they had walked on, Debby's two big brothers came pelting out of their house. "That was Mr. Jefferson and old Dr. Franklin!" they shouted. "They *spoke* to you. Don't you ever forget that!"

They were surprised that Debby didn't know the two men. They told her as best they could themselves, although when it came down to facts they found they didn't know as much as they thought.

3

Eagle Feathers and Tomahawks

Most Philadelphia families that year talked politics for breakfast, lunch, and supper. But not in the house where Debby lived. When an express rider brought in a piece of political news which raced through the city, Debby's mother looked worried and said nothing. Debby's father didn't seem worried a bit, but excited and eager. He looked as though he had a lot to say. But he never did say a word, because he didn't want to stir up an argument with his wife.

Once in a while his sons wanted to ask him to explain something they'd heard at school or in a schoolmate's home about the long dispute between the colonists and the English king. But they tried not to ask him where their mother could hear. They watched for him to come home, and ran to meet him a block away from the house.

But even then he didn't say much. He told them briefly what the facts were, and added, "Now your mother wouldn't want me to get you to take sides. She thinks so much of her Cousin John, you know."

"Cousin John" was Mr. John Dickinson. He was one of the Pennsylvania delegates to the Congress. A very fine man, so everybody said, even those who didn't agree with him about politics.

With all his heart, as hotly as John Adams wanted America to be entirely independent of England, John Dickinson wanted to remain a loyal subject of King George. That's what he said. He meant it too. But what he did was to vote money for more American Militia to make America strong to fight, exactly as if he were on the side of independence. He hated a real out-and-out Tory, whose idea was to take off his hat and make a bow and accept anything the king wanted to hand out. When Cousin John Dickinson met a British-minded person like that he flew into a rage, just as John Adams from Massachusetts did. Yet he always disagreed with Mr. Adams, and often very angrily.

The boys' mother, who knew her cousin well, said his point of view was easy to understand. He wanted to remain a loyal Englishman. But just *because* he had British ideas he wasn't going to be ordered around by anybody who didn't have a legal right to. He wanted an Englishman's full rights. His idea was, she said, that every Englishman knows you have to stand up for your rights if you don't want to have them taken away from you. Englishmen in England always had stood up for their rights. Look at the way they stood up against King Charles the First. If Englishmen in America showed that they were ready to right for their rights, they wouldn't have to. Cousin John felt that all this writing by Mr. Jefferson, for instance, about freedom and tyranny and whatnot, sounded to Great Britain like just talk.

"What the English government has always taken seriously and always will," he said, "is strength, not words. Make a fine speech about your never being willing to have your law cases tried in a court where the king has chosen the people in the jury, and nobody in the English Cabinet pays any attention to you. Reach for a loaded musket as you say it, and they'll give in peaceably to your reasons—if your reasons are good. And ours are good. They'll see we mean business. The stronger the colonies are in weapons and men, the surer we will be of getting our legal rights from England. It's always been that way with Englishmen. It always will be."

Just once the boys' father told them, after Cousin John Dickinson had been at the house talking like this, "Your mother's cousin is a fine man, but he doesn't realize that the man who is now king of England is more German than he is British. It hurts him so when anybody doesn't agree with him that he fairly yells with pain, the way a man yells with a toothache. The old English way was to respect people who disagree with you, if they are strong and reasonable. But King George hates such people! The

22

stronger they are, the more he hates them, because it makes him think for just an instant that there *might* be a possibility he couldn't always get his own way. And *that* idea seems to drive him just about crazy. But there, run along, boys. Your mother wouldn't like to have me talking to you like this. You are her sons as much as mine."

The boys got into a way of hanging around outside the front door of their house about the time their father was due home. They would pass a ball back and forth or play jackstones. But the minute they saw their father turn into the street three blocks away, they'd race to get to him.

"What's the news, Father, what happened today?" they would ask him in low voices, after they had reached him and were walking back, one on each side of him. Sometimes he didn't know any specially interesting news items. Sometimes the news was bad. That winter the American troops were fighting in Canada, trying to capture Canadian cities from the British, but they were badly beaten. They just couldn't get anywhere. That was terrible news.

Sometimes the news was exciting. Their father's voice was full of feeling on the days when he told them about one and then another and then another of the American colonies, where the British governor, appointed by the king, had left his office and taken refuge on an English warship. The people living in those colonies were now voting for their own governors, were choosing for themselves the men they wanted to run the government, instead of having to take any man the king wanted to send them. Connecticut people, for instance, had declared themselves no longer a British colony but a State, an American State, "under the sole authority of the people thereof, independent of any king or prince whatsoever."

"Now don't speak of this to your mother, boys. It would upset her. It's not what her Dickinson cousin believes should happen."

He himself evidently liked it fine. He said the words as if he loved every one of them. And another time, he choked up and had to stop talking for a minute because his heart was so full. This was when he had heard some young men from South Carolina talking about the day on which their newly elected governor—elected by the people's votes, not sent from England—and their assembly, also elected, marched to their State House.

"The South Carolina men told us the big crowds that gathered to watch the procession go by couldn't even cheer. They just stood 'in a kind of rapture,' men and women alike, to see, marching to music behind their escort of uniformed cadets, 'their *own* rulers, chosen by *them,* men they knew and loved and trusted. And men they themselves could vote out of office if they didn't do the right thing!' "

The boys never forgot the time—earlier in the year, in March—when their father told them, very much astonished, that the ten thousand red-coated British troops who had been in Boston all winter had sailed off to Canada.

The boys could scarcely believe their ears. Everybody had been afraid of what all those soldiers might do.

"*Why*? What made them go?" they asked their father.

"Well, the American troops got hold of the big cannons from Fort Ticonderoga, and put them on a hill across the water from Boston, where they could fire right into the city. But the British were about ready to leave anyhow. Starved out."

"But—but—but—" cried the older boy, "I thought the British Regulars could beat *any*body. Why did they *let* the Americans get the cannons up on the hill? Why didn't they march out and beat the American soldiers and just grab the food they wanted?"

"I can't imagine why not," said their father. "I don't know why any more than you do."

"Maybe the British Army isn't as good as they say it is?" ventured the older boy.

"Do you suppose that could be?" their father wondered. "It *does* seem very queer that they just backed off from the American Militia and went away. And I can't understand, either, why the English government didn't send food and muskets and gunpowder to supply their own army. They could have done it easily. The harbor of Boston is open to the sea. The English have got all the ships in creation. I can't make head or tail of it. But it sounds mighty good to all Americans. Unless there's a catch in it somewhere."

They were at the house now so they stopped talking and went in together.

It was understood between the boys that they were not to mention in the house these brief snatches of talk with their father.

But one piece of news they all enjoyed together, their mother as much as anybody else. The Congress had sent a special message to the Indians, asking them not to act as enemies to the English, not to attack the English if there should be fighting later on. They didn't ask them to support the Americans. The message said something like this: "What we are asking you for is *Peace*. This is not your quarrel. If it comes to fighting, the quarrel is between the colonists and Old England. It's not *your* fight at all. What we ask of you is to keep the hatchet buried deep."

The boys' mother talked a great deal about this. She told them to be proud of being English, not French. The French king had, she said, in those long-drawn-out French and Indian wars, *paid* the Indians good money to fight on his side. "They were paid, so I've always heard," she said, "a high price for every American colonist's scalp they could bring in."

"So you can see, boys," she ended her little talk, "how people act who are brought up in the English ideas of right and wrong. *Our* people *ask* the Indians *not* to attack *anybody*."

Congress did more than ask. They voted money to buy presents for the Indians to persuade them not to get into the fight. And, to the intense delight of Philadelphia children, after a while the six big Iroquois tribes sent word that more than twenty of their chieftains would come to the Continental Congress to thank the Americans for their gifts.

Debby and her brothers and her father and mother were all excited about this thank-you visit from real Indian chieftains. Their father found out which day the Indians were to come, May 28th it was, and which streets they would pass along to get to the State House. He said he would take the morning off and go with his family to see them.

Bright and early that day they stood waiting to see the Indians go by—along with crowds and crowds of other Philadelphia people.

"Mother, did you ever see Indians, real ones?" asked the boys as they waited on the sidewalk.

"Yes, once," she said. "When I was your age, I was taken to visit some family connections who lived way back country, in the woods. There were a few Indians around there. But they weren't much to see. They wore old, ragged white man's breeches and coats, with nothing more Indian-like than maybe a band of scarlet calico tied around their black hair."

The boys were disappointed. "Do you suppose these Indians will dress like that?" they asked.

Half an hour later they found out. From far away down the street came a low, dull, slow *throb, throb, throb*. It was a drum. Different from any drum they had ever heard.

People pushed the children into the front line so they could see. Everybody leaned forward and looked down the street.

Now, mingled with that dull throb from the drum, came a strange, dry rattle, like bones shaken together.

The chieftains were coming. Even from a distance you could tell they were Indians. Their copper-colored bodies were bare to the waist and painted in great staring patterns of many colors. With their every move their muscles rippled close under the skin—as they walked, as they breathed, as they swung their arms—so that the lines of the painted patterns stirred, writhed, seemed to be alive.

They wore short kilts and leggings of pale tan smoked buckskin, brilliantly decorated with bead embroidery which twinkled, flashed, caught the light in red and green and yellow and blue sparkles. Long belts fringed at the hanging ends. Sharp tomahawks thrust through those belts. And what footgear! Solid embroidery made of flat tiny quills, all colors woven in and out in patterns no white person knew how to make.

Over each head floated a single great eagle's feather. An elaborately decorated deerskin quiver filled with feathered arrows hung from the left shoulder to the right hip, across their backs. Most of them carried long, heavy bows. Some of them had in one hand a rattle made of turtle shells which they shook lightly in a faint, ghostly rhythm as they passed. Several wore legbands with dried deer-hooves hung closely together, dangling and rattling with a strange little noise unlike any other.

A gasp of wonder over these strange and gorgeous costumes went up from the Philadelphia crowd dressed in their own drab, substantial gray and brown clothes and thick-soled, practical black and brown shoes. But as the Indians went by, treading soundlessly in their soft-soled moccasins, a respectful silence fell on those American colonists.

The bright-colored embroideries, the muffled sounds from drum and rattles—they were forgotten once the warriors came stepping by, their thin, bleak faces focused on something far, far away. They might have been walking, each by himself, on a lonely path in the woods. The sight was never forgotten by the children who, that day, gazed up into those high-nosed, stonelike, copper-skinned faces with the long black locks hanging on each side. They were mighty fighting men, every one of them. But they went by like shadows, with a step as noiseless as a deer's.

People forgot they had come out to see a show. They stood silent, almost shy in the presence of such an impressive group.

On the way home the boys said not a word. Their

4

Common Sense

The snatches of talk the boys had with their father were short. And he always reminded them that he didn't know about anything for sure. Especially about what was going on in the Continental Congress. The delegates had promised not to tell anybody about the discussions of the Congress. But of course everybody wondered, speculated, gossiped, and then passed on these guesses and rumors. Yet everybody knew well enough that they were only guesses.

But the boys often wondered what the delegates did all day long, every single day except Sunday, all through the hot summer, and the mild Pennsylvania autumn, and the dark winter days, and the spring again, almost to summer. The boys just could not imagine what those men found to do all that time, behind those closed doors, sitting round in chairs, talking and talking.

Their father always told them he didn't like to discuss politics at home because he and their mother had such different ideas, and he didn't like to disagree with her. Yet the children knew their parents couldn't keep off the subject which, that year, filled everybody's thoughts. They knew their father and mother *did* talk about it together, for after they had gone to bed they often heard those two voices going on and on downstairs in the living room. But since the day they had had that dispute about *Common Sense*—well, it wasn't perhaps a real dispute, but it came as close to that as anything that had ever happened in that home—the boys had known their father didn't want *them* to get their mother started about independence and King George III, and the Continental Congress, and all the rest that was being discussed over and over in everybody else's house.

What had happened about that book was this: one morning in February, the master of the boys' school had walked into the classroom reading a little paper-covered pamphlet. He laid it on his desk, but as he took off his hat and heavy coat he leaned over it, reading fast, as though he couldn't stop. And then, sitting down, he raced through a page or two before he remembered where he was and called the school to order.

The boys near his desk craned their necks, of course, and caught a glimpse or two of the pages. They did not look a bit interesting. No pictures. No conversation. Just solid fine print, like a school textbook. But when he finally closed it, they could read the title—*Common Sense*. Of all things to get excited about! Yet all that day their teacher, whenever he was not busy with a class reciting a lesson, snatched the little book up and read in it. While they did their arithmetic problems, they kept flicking quick glances at him, because as he read his face grew flushed, his eyes sparkled and blazed. Several times he laughed out loud, and once he clenched one hand into a fist and brought it down, slam! on his desk. It made them jump.

And how it did make them want to know what was inside that dull-looking book with that dull title. "Common sense" was something your grandparents lectured you about, and very tiresome they made it sound. They were on pretty good terms with their teacher, and before they went home that afternoon they gathered around his desk to ask him about the book.

"Oh, did you notice I was reading something?" he asked them, surprised.

"Tell us about it! Can we read it?" they asked. "Will you read it to us?"

He thought for a minute, then said, "I declare I don't know. Your parents may have different ideas from mine." He hesitated. "I tell you what," he suggested, "you ask your parents this evening if they're willing to have you read *Common Sense*. Then you tell me tomorrow morning. I'll lend it to any boy whose folks say he may read it. You don't need me or anybody else to read it to you. It's

33

easy—reads itself—like somebody talking to you."

"But how can we ask them if we don't know what it's about? How can they know what kind of a book it is if you don't give us some idea?" they asked him.

To their surprise, he laughed heartily at this. "You'll find your folks will know about it, all right," he told them.

And *did* they! That evening at the supper table the older of Debby's brothers said, "Say, Father, Teacher was reading a book today called *Common Sense*—"

Their mother dropped her knife and fork on her plate with a clatter. "Did he read that book *to you*?" she asked in an angry-sounding voice.

No, no, they assured her. He had been reading it to himself, and they noticed he seemed all taken up with it, so they asked him if they could read it. And he said to ask their families if they could.

"Certainly not!" said their mother. "You're much too young. I won't have your minds upset."

The boys turned to their father. He shook his head. "I don't want you children to go against your mother's wishes," he told them. "The book really is for grownups anyhow."

"Now listen to me," said their mother seriously. "I want you to promise you won't look inside that book. You always keep your promises, I know."

"But how would we ever have a chance *to* look inside it," they asked, bewildered, "if we're not allowed to see Teacher's copy?"

At this, their father and mother looked oddly at each

other. Suddenly the boys got the idea that there must be a copy of the book in their own house. After all, if their mother hadn't read it, how would she know, at the first mention of its title, that she didn't want *them* to read it?

Their father said, smiling a little as though there was a joke they didn't know, "You *may* see other copies. Your teacher may not be the only one to have the book."

"But, *Mother*—" they began imploringly.

Their father said quickly and a little sharply, "Now boys, I want you to promise. Your mother does everything in the world for you. It won't kill you—just not to read one book. It'll be right there for you to read later on, when you're older. Now promise."

So they promised. They thought a lot of their mother, and they knew it was not easy for her to disagree with their father.

They kept their promise too. As their mother said, they always did. But it was hard. In a few days that little paper-covered book seemed to be everywhere. They knew now why their father had been amused by their thinking their teacher's would be the only copy they would see. Every house seemed to contain a copy. People read it as they walked along the streets. Newspaper articles about other things would suddenly say, "As *Common Sense* remarks. . . ." The man who lived next door leaned over the wall between the two backyards and read a piece out of it to their father as he was planting the peas. In the bakery, or at the greengrocer's shop when their mother sent them on errands, they heard people talking about it.

So although they did not once look inside the book (till their mother gave them leave to), they couldn't help knowing some of the things that were in it. Since they did not see the words, they didn't get them just the way they were printed. But they got the sense of those sayings. Nobody who had once heard them could forget them. This is the way they remembered some of the things people were quoting to each other that winter:

"In England the king hath little more to do than to make war and hand out easy jobs for rich people to make them richer. A pretty business, for a man to be allowed four million dollars a year for that—and to expect to be worshipped into the bargain!"

"Trace back a king's forefathers—the head of his family was always the strongest thief in a band of robbers."

"England calls itself our 'mother country'! Not much! Europe, not England, is the father and mother of America. This new world hath been a safe home for people from every part of Europe who want to live in Freedom."

"England hath given Freedom warning to depart. Oh, America, receive Freedom, and prepare a place for men to live in liberty!"

They began to understand why their mother didn't want them to read that book! But she was wrong about it upsetting their minds. It didn't. They agreed with what it said.

5

Report to Debby

All that winter and spring, one British colony after another was voting itself into an American State. Like their father, the boys felt proud of each new State governor, chosen by the people, not sent from England to do what the king told him to.

At the table the family talked about the weather, and lame Aunt Ann's rheumatism, and wondered when the first strawberries would be ripe in their garden. But by themselves, the boys kept on wondering aloud about the doings of the delegates to the Continental Congress. What did those men do all day long, they asked each other. What went on behind those closed doors week after week? With almost every colony declaring itself independent of England, why didn't *they*—representing all the colonies as they did—do something like that for the whole of America?

Their little sister Debby was often playing around near them as they talked together. But they paid no attention to her. They didn't think she would be interested in what they were saying.

But Debby had heard her brothers repeat the same questions so often that by the end of the first year after the delegates had come to Philadelphia the words had stuck fast in her memory like a counting-out rhyme.

She had an idea that what her brothers asked so often had something to do with the stout old gentleman who sometimes walked slowly past her home with the slim, elegantly dressed young gentleman who had a little girl at home named Patsy, just about Debby's size. Old Dr. Franklin was dreadfully lame. He leaned all his weight on Mr. Jefferson's arm.

One day in June, when little Debby saw the two delegates coming near, she suddenly laid her doll on the grass and ran to meet them, calling out, "What do you do, all day long, every day? What do you *do*?"

The two men stopped, astonished. Then they laughed. Mr. Jefferson sat down on his heels till he was Debby's size and asked, "Say that again, Debby, won't you?"

Debby was much too young to feel shy. So she repeated it, looking straight at him, her blue eyes wide. Dr. Franklin said, smiling, "Tom, what Debby asks must be an echo of what *everybody* is asking."

Mr. Jefferson stood up. "But what in the world can you

tell a little girl like Debby?" he asked, stroking the silky hair that was like his little Patsy's.

But old Dr. Franklin pointed to a stone mounting block near them. "Debby, climb up, will you, dear, so you and I will each be as tall as the other, and I'll tell you something."

Debby scrambled up like a squirrel and stood there, her bright little face on a level with Dr. Franklin's. He took her tiny hand in his wrinkled, knotty old fingers.

"You may be too little to understand *now*," he said, "and we can't really tell you anyhow, not *really,* because we've promised not to. But we can give you an idea. If you'll be here when we pass by tomorrow afternoon, I'll have a report for you."

Mr. Jefferson lifted the little girl down and shook her hand. "Don't forget," he said. "Tomorrow afternoon."

The two delegates walked on. Debby went to pick up her doll. Out of the house rushed her two brothers.

"For goodness' *sakes!*" they cried. "Whatever in the world did you say to them? And what did they say to you?"

"Why, I asked them what they do all day long, every day. And they said they'd tell me tomorrow."

The two boys didn't believe her, and they took Debby in to their mother.

She was as much astonished as they. She thought, as they did, that Debby had probably gotten something twisted.

"I believe I'd better be out there with her tomorrow

afternoon," she said. "I'm afraid my little girl has been forward. I don't want her to bother people, even if she didn't mean to."

"Oh, Mother, may we be there too?" the boys asked.

"Why not?" she said. "If you're quiet, and mind your manners."

So the next afternoon all of Debby's family—except her father—stood there with her when Dr. Franklin and Mr. Jefferson came along. Debby's mother had made them practice their manners. When the delegates were near, she herself spread out her wide skirts and bowed low in a dipping curtsy. The boys bent over from the waist in a bow. Debby wore long full skirts, too, and her mother had showed her how to spread them out to make a curtsy. But just as she took hold of them, old Dr. Franklin smiled. It was his good, grandfatherly smile. His pale, wrinkled old face looked desperately tired. But his smile was like sunshine. Debby forgot her manners and ran to him, her arms wide open—clasping him around his knees.

The two gentlemen took off their cocked hats, bowed to Debby's mother, and gave a friendly nod to the boys. Mr. Jefferson said, holding out a piece of paper, "Here, little miss, is our report."

Things were written on the paper—letters and figures. Debby ran back to her mother with it. "Oh, read it to me! Read it to me!" she cried.

"Yes, do, madam," said Mr. Jefferson. "The paper is for

the little American to keep. Someday she will understand it."

He swept off his three-cornered hat and made a fine bow. Dr. Franklin felt in his pocket, brought out a piece of sugar candy, and slipped it into Debby's hand. They went on. Debby's mother stood with the paper in her hand, blinking her eyes.

"What's on it, Mother?" asked the boys.

"Let's go into the house to read it," she said, "where we can be quiet."

Inside the house, she read the paper through to herself. When she had finished, she looked doubtfully at her sons. "I don't know what to do about this," she said in a troubled voice.

"Oh, let us see what's on it!" cried the boys.

Debby had wandered away, her doll in her arms. As she sucked on Dr. Franklin's sugar candy, she thought that was much the best part of what had happened.

"I don't know whether I ought to," said their mother.

"Oh, Mother, why not!" they begged. "*All* the other boys' folks tell them about everything. Why shouldn't we—?"

She put the paper into her pocket. "Let me discuss it with your father first," she told them.

6

Under the Pear Tree in the Garden

Their father came home rather late for supper, as he often did in those days. The boys thought he looked tired and worried and yet excited. Little Debby had already had her bowl of bread and milk and gone to bed. She and her doll were sound asleep. Supper was eaten quietly. The boys had agreed not to tell their father about the "Report to Debby" till he had had his supper and lighted his pipe. They waited till they had all gone out to the walled-in garden plot back of the house, to sit under the pear tree in the mild Philadelphia early summer evening.

When their mother, with a nod, gave the boys leave to say what they were bursting to tell, their words tumbled over one another.

"Take turns, take turns," said their mother. "First one, then the other."

They told their story, then said, "We want to *ask* you about it!"

"Let me see this paper," their father said, holding out his hand. "As you tell it, it's nonsense. The delegates are under the strictest orders not to let a word of their proceedings—" He held out his hand. They gave him the paper.

He read it all through carefully, laid it down on his knees, took his pipe out of his mouth, and turned to his wife. He spoke gently, as they had always heard him speak to their mother, but he said something they had never heard him say before. "I think, Wife, that boys as big as ours ought to know what's going on."

The mother said earnestly, "But I want them to hear what I think, too."

The father nodded. "Yes. That's fair." He turned his eyes on the boys very seriously. "But listen," he said, "no nonsense about this. I'll answer your questions as well as I can, but I won't guarantee you'll find it interesting. Dr. Franklin probably thought of this as a little piece of foolery to amuse Debby. It's said that he spoils his grandchildren terribly."

He read out:

" 'Report to a young American on the kind of work done by the Second Continental Congress, all day long, every day, as she says. Set down in the month of June 1776 for Debby, by two fellow Americans slightly older than she.

" 'Every day, about two-and-one-half hours spent listening to letters from the Colonies . . . reports on their status.' "

The father laid the paper down a moment to say, "The word *status* means how they are getting along. Of course we all know that reports are received. We've eyes in our heads. Express riders come and go all the time, and every stableboy knows where they come from."

He went on:

" 'Often, of late, debate on the best means to comply with General Washington's request for longer enlistments.' "

The father sighed. "We know that, too—worse luck! For a while last winter, so many three-months-Militia soldiers went home that the general could hardly find men to hold his lines before Boston."

He read on from the paper:

" 'Lengthy consideration of the state of our Treasury . . . after which we vote—

" 'To authorize purchase of muskets for one battalion, and to authorize purchase of uniforms, provided the cost be deducted from the soldiers' pay.

" 'To authorize payment of twenty-three dollars for cartridge making.

" 'To authorize payment of twelve dollars to nurse for soldiers with smallpox.

" 'We listen to reports from various committees, such as Service of the Constitutional Post.
Saltpeter.
Ways and Means to Protect Trade of the Colonies.

Board of War and Ordnance.

" 'You see, Debby, many things concern *all* United Colonies, not just Pennsylvania and Virginia, and such things we, the Congress of those United Colonies, have to take care of. We are trying to run your country's business for you just as your mother runs your home. Dull, tiresome details are always part of the work of government, as of housekeeping. They must be thought about, and talked about, and decided honestly and promptly, even though they are not at all interesting.

" 'Remember this, my dear child, when you are a woman grown and living under a free government of your own people.

" 'The great things do not come by themselves. They are built up by working hard to solve the tiresome little problems which come up, day after day.' "

Respectfully submitted,

B. FRANKLIN

T. JEFFERSON

The father laid the paper down on his knee, took up his pipe, and said, "Now, boys, what is it you want to ask me?"

The younger one had his question on the tip of his tongue, and got it out before his brother could open his mouth. "What in the world is saltpeter? Why should the Congress have a committee about that?"

Their father found this an easy one. "We must have gunpowder. It's made of three things mixed together—charcoal, sulfur, and saltpeter. Anybody can make charcoal. And sulfur isn't hard to get. But saltpeter! It's hard to find. And to make. There *are* places where it is found in the earth. It can be bought from such places. But it costs a lot.

"Now, England has any amount of money. The same year they got hold of Canada from the French, they also got hold of India. India is a big, rich country. Lots of money comes into England from there. More than that, England is full of manufacturers, and they pay taxes by the hatful. The king can get plenty of money to buy saltpeter anywhere in the world. But we can't."

The older boy asked, "What kind of manufacturers are those in England that pay so many taxes?"

"All kinds," said the father. "Woolen goods—iron-works—plating mills. Hats."

"Why don't we have them manufactured here in America, and get taxes from them?"

"Because the British government won't let us," said their father promptly. "Their idea is to keep us from manufacturing things for ourselves. That would make us prosperous. They don't think anybody should be as prosperous as people born in England. Take hats. Beaver hats are all the style. There's lots of money in manufacturing them from beaver skins. All the beavers are on this side of the Atlantic Ocean. None in England. Americans are 'allowed' to trap the beavers. But if we make hats out of the fur, we are not 'allowed' to sell them where the British hatmakers want to do business.

"And take wool. Our wives and mothers are 'allowed'

to spin and weave homespun cloth inside our own homes. But if you live in Pennsylvania, you are not 'allowed' to sell a yard of it across the river in New Jersey. And of course none of it must be sold in England, or Holland, or France. The English woolmakers want to sell in those countries. There's money in selling good woolen cloth. So only the English can do it.

"And iron foundries. The English are glad to have us send heavy bar iron across the ocean to them. Rough iron by itself isn't worth much. Then they make all kinds of useful things out of our iron and ship them. We could do it here as well as they. But they make laws to forbid it to Americans.

"Take nails! The first step is to cut big chunks of iron into little pieces in a slitting mill. The pieces can be made into nails in home forges. Our farmers would like to do this in winter. But the British law forbids our setting up any new slitting mills. So our countrymen have to sit idle when farm work is slack. British manufacturers can make money out of nails, so nobody else must be allowed to do it."

The boys' mother spoke now, in a low murmur. "I may be only a housewife, but I know as well as you that there is a lot of ironwork done in Pennsylvania."

"That's true," admitted their father, "and there are lots of hat factories in New England. And all of them, if they were started since that British law was made, are illegal." He turned to the boys. "You are not in manufacturing, of course, so you don't know what crooked business a man is forced into if he runs a factory forbidden by English law. There are, of course, certain officials who ought to report you. You have to bribe them not to do it. You have to bribe anybody who threatens to tell on you. The officials you bribe have to bribe others to keep it quiet. It means dishonesty in everything you do. It means the whole machinery of enforcing the law gets rotten. And why? So that British manufacturers can make money.

"Now to go back to saltpeter. Dr. Franklin is one of the finest scientists anywhere. I'm pretty sure he is on the committee to see what can be done about saltpeter. I hear too that up in New England some of their best people are working on that problem. If we can't get saltpeter, we're beaten before we start."

The older boy broke in with a question. "That committee to protect the trade of the colonies—why should it have to be protected?"

His father snorted, rather as if the question rubbed him the wrong way. "Not much chance of protecting it as things stand nowadays. We haven't got much to protect."

"What's the matter with it?"

"Well, in the first place, the British government has never *allowed* us to trade with any country but England. We have never been *allowed* to buy anything direct from France, or Holland, or Italy. Yet people in those countries make lots of things we'd be glad to buy from them. The English government has always *ordered* us to buy everything through English merchants. *They* can buy wherever they like, and they are very glad to sell to us. At a profit, of course. Almost any profit they want, since we *have* to buy from them."

Their mother said nothing. She was knitting a pair of stockings for Debby and kept her eyes on her work.

"And now it's worse," their father went on. "They've gone further. They used to *allow* us to trade only with them. But now the king, since he is so angry with Massachusetts and all the rest of us Americans, won't let *any* trade go on, in and out of our ports. Last winter he announced to the rest of the world that we are rebels and that nobody, anywhere, is to buy anything from us or sell us anything, or he will consider *them* enemies. In the same announcement he told the world that any American ship could be captured at sea by anybody who wanted to capture it, its cargo taken, and its sailors made prisoners, and *he* wouldn't care, because he has no use for us. As long as we keep on being British colonies, there's nothing we can do about that. But if we declare ourselves an independent country—"

The boys looked quickly at their mother. She looked very serious as she murmured, "They'll never, never vote for independence," but she let their father continue.

"—We can buy things from anywhere, except England, of course, and sell them to any country. I suppose this committee to protect the trade of the colonies has something to do with that."

The older boy reached over, took up the "Report to Debby," and ran his eyes over it. "What's this about a Board of War and Ordnance?" he asked.

His father hesitated a moment and his mother laid down her knitting. "I think *my* turn has come to speak," she said. "That committee is working to get everything ready to make war on England. Your father has been explaining the reasons. Because we think they are making more than their fair share of money. Because we think we could make more money if we were independent of them. Just business. But decent people don't try to kill each other over money. They do it legally, not with gunmen. Your father doesn't take a loaded musket downtown and shoot a man because he's making more money than we are—even if your father thinks he is not exactly fair. He tries his best under the law to make the man do the right thing." She spoke quietly, with no excitement.

Their father said, "I'm so glad you are willing to talk this over together. With our sons. It's been a sorrow to me to have anything between us that we can't talk about. It is important for our boys to learn that people can have different ideas and still not be angry with one another."

He put his hand on hers and asked, "May I go on?"

She nodded. But just before he spoke again, she said with deep feeling, "Our Congress will never vote for independence. That would mean war. It won't come to shooting. It can't. There are too many good folk in England who don't want war any more than we do."

Her husband said gently, "Yes, so there are. But just now our kind of people in England don't have—so it seems—much to say about running their government. And we *have* war now. The shooting started last April, in Lexington and Concord. And in June at Bunker Hill."

"We must keep it from spreading beyond Massachusetts," she said in a low voice. "The king will send us people to make peace, not war—*if we are patient.* That is what Cousin John Dickinson keeps saying. If we show we are in earnest, they will send people to get all these tangles straightened. I expect every day that express riders from New York will come in with that news."

Her husband thought a long time before he answered her. "Your cousin John Dickinson is a fine man. He is sure that we could, if we would only go on trying, get together with the English people. But we can't reach the English people. Between us stands this king. He's managed to get the government entirely into the hands of his friends. And they all have the same idea he has—or they wouldn't be friends of his."

"What is his idea?" asked the older boy.

"It's what's called 'personal rule.' That means 'The king is the master.' It's a very old idea that was given up in England long, long ago—that ordinary people who work every day for their living should have mighty little right to say what their government does. The king wants to go back to the old days, when anybody who could get himself onto a throne felt he could do whatever he pleased. He's very stubborn, and he's kept at it and *kept* at it, till now he's got the government in England under his thumb.

"Your mother isn't quite fair in saying that what we are ready to fight for is only the right to make more money. It's the right to live under law, not under some man's orders. And we think that law is made by everybody's getting together and deciding what has to be done."

Their mother said, "But the king has *said* that he is going to send over some fine, upright people to make peace with us."

"That's what he *said*," answered her husband, "but what did he do? Sent over ships with cannon and attacked Falmouth in Maine and Norfolk in Virginia, places with no forts and no artillery to fight back—just a lot of homes with families in them—and burned those cities to the ground. And his orders were—we know this for sure—to attack our seacoast cities 'at that time of year when it would most distress the people who live in them.' "

His wife did not contradict this, but she murmured, "We must be patient. There are always misunderstandings. It is wrong to take for granted that a misunderstanding—"

"There's no misunderstanding about the king's hating us," said her husband, his voice rising a little. "He hates us because we stand for everybody here or in England or Scotland who won't give in to him on everything. It won't be people to make peace with us that he'll send over.

He'll send—why, the talk around town is that he's going to pay thousands and thousands of foreign soldiers to fight us!"

His wife cried out, "The English people would never let the king do such a thing."

"He's got them where they can't help it."

"That's the craziest story I ever heard!" exclaimed his wife.

"Yes, it does sound like wild talk," admitted the father, "but I keep hearing it."

The younger boy yawned. Their mother's eye caught this. She stood up. "There, I think we've talked enough for tonight."

It was dark. A little moon showed through the branches of the pear tree. They went back into the house and each one lighted a candle to carry up to bed. On the wall, King George's face looked out at them from over the fireplace where his picture had always hung.

7

Debby's Mother Changes Her Mind

After the talk under the pear tree, Debby's brothers felt that their father treated them more like men. He talked to them more about the danger of British ships someday appearing in the river, close at hand, and shooting up Philadelphia as they had shot and burned down other American cities. He told them more about what he was doing, serving in the guard set to protect Philadelphia.

On the evening of the last day of June, their father asked them to take a walk with him. Their mother took for granted that they were just going out for a stroll, leaving her to put Debby to bed.

As soon as they were out of the house their father said in an anxious voice, "Now, boys, there's something on my mind. Let's go around to those benches near the State House yard. We can talk there without anybody hearing us. It's about your mother. You know what your mother thinks about England, and how Americans ought to act."

Yes, the boys said, they knew how their mother felt.

"That evening under the pear tree, you remember how she simply would not believe that the king might pay foreigners to fight in the English army. She said it was foolishness to think he would take millions of dollars from the British taxpayers to *buy* himself an army to get the better of us Americans. She said it was just gossip. She said you could hear anything."

Yes, the boys remembered that very well.

"Well, he's done it," said their father in a heavy, desperate voice. "Your mother hasn't heard the news yet. But it's all over town. It's not just talk anymore. News has come in from General Washington himself that more than a hundred British ships—oh, many more than a hundred—have been sighted coming into New York harbor. Lots of them are warships, armed with cannon. They could shoot New York City right off the map. And Philadelphia, too. If they could get up the river.

"Those that aren't fighting ships are transports, full of soldiers. A *big* army. The biggest that ever crossed the Atlantic. The English soldiers are Regulars mostly, paid professionals. Such troops fight to earn their living. They'll attack anybody, anytime, anywhere, because that's their business. But the king hasn't nearly enough professional soldiers to put down the Americans. So he's taken in thousands of Highland Scottish and Irish troops.

Where those people live, everybody is kept so very poor, the men have to take any job they can get to keep from starving."

He took a long breath. "And boys, nine thousand hired German soldiers are landing. And ever so many more thousands coming in later. The king's going to bring over thirty thousand Hessians. More than we have in all our American armies put together. He'll pay more than fifteen million dollars to those German kings or princes before he gets through. He'll pay *any*thing (only of course it's not out of *his* pocket, it's tax money paid by the British people) and do anything to punish Americans because we want to have our fair legal rights, as the British law gives us rights."

"Oh, what'll Mother *think*!" exclaimed the older boy.

"Will she have to know?" asked the younger.

"Of course she will. She'd have known by now if she were talking to businessmen out on the street. Everybody's been talking about it. But that's not all." He paused, took off his hat, wiped his forehead, swallowed hard. "There's something worse."

Now the boys were frightened. What could be worse?

"At least those Germans are soldiers. They fight other soldiers, not women and children. But the king is going to give the Indians leave to burn American homes and kill American families, to help him get the better of us. The *English* king! And he used to talk so against the French for having the Indians fight beside them and murder white settlers."

The boys were too shocked to speak. They stared silently at their father. What would their mother say about this when she heard the news? She would be so upset, so disappointed in the king.

Finally the older boy said in a low voice, "Mother certainly didn't seem to like the looks of those Indians when we went to see them."

Their father nodded. "Your mother has good reason to be worried about Indians. She has never told you this, but one of her uncles was killed in a French and Indian raid. So were all his family—his wife and three little children. We'll have to try our best to make her understand that this is not something for her to worry about here in Philadelphia."

It was almost dark when their father drew a long breath and got up from the bench where they had been sitting.

"I wanted you to know this, boys," he said, "before your mother heard the news. I thought all three of us could be more of a comfort to her if you knew beforehand."

The big bell in the State House tower slowly struck eight. "We'd better go back now."

On the way home, none of them said a word. They walked slowly.

As they approached the house, they saw that candles had been lighted in the front room. And the curtains had not been drawn together! Their mother always drew the curtains or closed the shutters before she lighted a candle. Everybody did in those days. Through the unveiled windows they could see her pacing rapidly to and fro in the room. Startled, the boys ran to fling open the door. She heard them coming and spun around to face them. They had never seen her look so tall.

The instant she saw them she began to speak.

"While you were gone, news came in," she told them in a strange, low, sharp voice that sent shivers up their backs. "You must hear it too. Express riders are in from New York. They say an enormous fleet of British warships has come into that harbor. They are bringing a tremendous army. All the British Regulars who were shut up in Boston. Other Regulars. And thousands and thousands of German soldiers! More than a million dollars of British taxpayers' money is to be paid for their hire."

Her voice deepened, darkened. "And the king, our English king, is not just sending soldiers to fight our soldiers. He is going to use unfriendly Indians to attack us, just as the French did."

She was trembling now, but her burning eyes showed that it was from anger, not fear. "It makes me *ashamed*," she cried, "to have been a subject of a king who will do that. Why, what have we done that he should want to burn our houses and slaughter our children! We have disagreed with him about taxes. The quarrel is about *money*! Would I, if I could, send hired soldiers and Indians along the country roads in England just to get the better of them in a quarrel about *taxes*! I'd die before I would. And so would any decent person."

She flung back her head. "The king won't even read our petitions to send people to arrange this in peace. His only answer is to send over the biggest army that ever crossed the ocean to kill us, and the biggest fleet to burn what's left of our seacoast cities."

She flung out her arm and cried, "He thinks he can *scare* us into taking less than our legal rights. Why, he's just a bully!"

Stepping close to her husband, she cried, "Now we must never give up, never! Never! Now the Congress *must* vote for independence. Now they will!"

She turned to her sons who were gaping, astonished by her change of heart. "Boys, *nobody* must *ever* give in to a bully because he has a big club! This is more than a quarrel between two countries. It's between what makes life worth living and what makes you ashamed to be alive. In that fight, if the bullies come out on top just because they are strong, it will be shame, shame for everybody—everywhere, forever! Never forget that, my sons."

They ran to her and put their arms around her. Over their heads, she said to her husband passionately, "If I could, I'd shoulder a musket and go out to fight alongside you."

"Well!" said their father. He hadn't even taken his hat off yet. He did now. Holding it in his hands, he bowed before his wife, lifted her hand in his, and kissed her fingers.

She looked lovingly around at their three faces. She

tried to smile. But she could not smile. Not yet. She had something else to say. She spoke very earnestly. "You're thinking I'm going back on everything I've told you before. Not a bit. I don't want to fight the English nation, and they don't want to fight us. If *they* were the ones who wanted to fight us, this army landing in New York would be made up of enlisted Englishmen, not of starving Highlanders and Irish, of professional soldiers and Germans. The very reason the king has to *buy* himself an army is because his own people won't fight us. Never forget that, boys."

She sat down in her own small armchair, where the boys had so often sat on her lap when they were little. She had one last thing to say.

"Nobody knows what's before us," she told them. "We may not often be together by ourselves like this. There is one thing I want you to remember, no matter what comes. When we are threatened by a bully, why do we flare up and stand fast instead of being afraid and giving up? It is because our forefathers came from England. It's not against the English people I'm ready to have my country fight. It's *for* them. Maybe the king has got *them* down where they can't flare up and stand fast, as they always used to, but he hasn't got *us Americans* down. If these are years when they can't fight, as they did a hundred years ago, against a king who wants to run the government all by himself, well, we'll do it. It's our turn."

Now the boys and their father sat down too. It seemed

a lot longer than one short hour since they had left this cozy room for their talk on the bench.

But something was different. Something was changed. Dazed and shaken, they looked vaguely around them. What could have changed in such a short time?

Their mother was speaking to them again. They turned back to her. "Mercy!" she said. "It's way past your bedtime. What are we thinking of! You won't be able to stay awake at school tomorrow. Be off with you! Don't forget to hang up your clothes, and wash your feet, and say your prayers before you get into bed."

They went up to their rooms, clumpingly, their heavy shoes loud on the stairs.

As they reached the top their mother called after them, "Boys! you might as well read *Common Sense* now, if you want to. It's in the chest of drawers in our bedroom. Third from the top. Left-hand side. Under my stockings."

As they undressed one said to the other in a hushed voice, "Did you notice? The picture of King George is gone from over the fireplace."

The other nodded. "Yes, I saw it standing in the corner with its face to the wall."

They gazed wide-eyed at each other, shook their heads, and fell into bed.

8

Let Freedom Ring!

Debby's mother was right. The Congress did vote for independence. Philadelphia was now so full of talk about who was voting which way in Congress that nobody had breath for anything else.

Not that anybody knew anything for certain. The delegates were not supposed to breathe a word about their discussions to anyone. And they didn't. Not really. But everybody was so wrought up that news seemed to leak out through the mortar and bricks of the State House walls. Maybe none of it was true, people would say to each other, even while they were repeating what they had heard. And there was plenty of rumor.

Everywhere they went they heard reports of what was going on.

"It seems a Virginia delegate stood right up there in

the State House and moved that the colonies are, and of right ought to be, free and independent!"

"It was 'most a month ago he said that, but they haven't voted on it yet."

"It will be voted any day now."

"No, it won't. John Dickinson is working just as hard as ever against breaking off from England. He says he's ready to enlist in General Washington's army and fight for our legal rights. But no independence for him. He wants us to stay British. He's a stubborn man."

"He won't change. And I'll wager the other Pennsylvania delegates will back him up."

"Maryland's against it too."

"They *were* against it. Their legislature is meeting again. I've heard that they're going to send different instructions."

Then, somehow, the word got around that John Adams of Massachusetts had made a wonderful speech in favor of independence. It wasn't any surprise to have him urge separation from Great Britain. What astonished people was his intense, burning feeling about it. He had been thought rather cold by nature. He often walked alone on the Philadelphia streets, always sober-faced and tight-lipped. People thought he was not friendly-looking. And he was a lawyer who, like most lawyers, was a good man in an argument. But this speech of his was no legal argument with pros and cons. It was a fiery outpouring from his heart of love for human freedom and hatred for what stood in the way of human freedom. Nobody could resist it. Why—it was said—the delegates were fairly lifted out of their chairs by it, cheering and applauding—yes, even those who had always said they were going to vote no.

"I don't guarantee this to be true, neighbor, but it's what I hear. They say he made John Dickinson with his cautious, British-leaning speech sound like a sick old cat."

"But Delaware is in a snarl. It has only two delegates in Philadelphia, and they take different sides."

"Now, Cousin Peter, we're all guessing. Nothing's known."

"But some say that their third delegate, Caesar Rodney, will vote yes. Then Delaware's vote would be two to one, in favor of independence."

"Maybe, but poor Rodney's a sick man, and eighty miles away down in South Delaware."

"No hope of getting him here in time."

But there was. An express rider was sent out with a letter calling him back to vote. And Caesar Rodney answered the call. He tied a green silk handkerchief over his face to hide the scars of his disease, and wore out four changes of horses as he galloped all night through the dark, over muddy roads, with July thunderstorms rolling wildly about his head.

The little knot of watchers on Chestnut Street never, till their dying day, forgot the mud-spattered horse and rain-soaked rider, the tall, skeleton-thin man, his face masked up to his hollow, sunken eyes. He was so stiff from that tremendous ride that he had to be helped out of the saddle. For an instant he swayed on his feet. He almost fell. Then he went up the steps and into the door of the State House.

People turned to one another and said, "That was Rodney. Delaware will be all right now."

And how about Pennsylvania? Had anybody seen John Dickinson that day? Was he inside the hall? It turned out that he wasn't. Debby's mother had been wrong in thinking that Hessians and Indians in the British army would change his vote. But only partly wrong. Even now he couldn't give up his dream of convincing the king to grant the legal rights of Englishmen everywhere. He still had a vision of an America ruled with justice, where no one would be taxed without representation. But he wanted it to be British justice. He couldn't bring himself to vote to break away from England. But in the end he didn't vote against independence either. He and a friend who thought as he did stayed away. And Pennsylvania, together with all the other colonies, said yes. The Declaration of Independence was voted.

People still spoke of them as "colonies" more than half the time, though that wasn't exactly accurate. All of them now by the will of their own citizens had declared themselves States—all except New York, which hadn't quite finished doing that. But its yes vote was promised as soon as it too had finished changing itself over from a British colony to an American State.

All thirteen "colonies" were now States, dependent on

the votes of their own people, not on the king or his ministers. They could now join together as one nation, and as one nation declare to the whole world their union and their independence.

At last the people of Philadelphia could stop guessing. The great question was settled. The Declaration officially adopted was to be read aloud inside the high walls around the State House yard at noon. People began planning to be there early.

In Debby's home, the evening before that great day, there was a long discussion. The little girl was to be left at home, her parents said. Lame old Aunt Ann could come in to stay with her.

But Debby's brothers said she must go too. "Why, she's the one Dr. Franklin and Mr. Jefferson first spoke to. And now people say those two are the ones who've written the Declaration mostly. It would be too mean to leave *her* at home."

The father saw the boys' point. "There's something in what they say," he said. "It'll be a great thing for anybody to say—that he heard, with his own ears, the first public reading of the Declaration of Independence."

They set off early. Not any too early. The yard was big, but long before noon it was not big enough. The crowd grew denser. Debby's father held her on his shoulder. The boys stood on each side of their mother, each one holding fast to her hand, not to be separated from her.

Around them people were inching themselves into less space.

Some time ago, a wooden platform had been put up in the yard for looking at the stars. A rough little wooden building called the observatory had been left on it. And somehow Debby's family found they had been slowly pushed by the crowd into a position where their view was hidden by the observatory.

The boys felt that this was too much to bear.

"Now, Father! It's not *fair*! We were here first. We ought to—"

Their father showed them with a motion of his hand that nobody could move, not an inch, from where he stood. He said, "We didn't come to see, but to hear."

Just then a man behind them began to say something about the bell in the State House. The boys strained their ears to hear what was being said. "That bell was ordered from England to celebrate the fiftieth anniversary of William Penn's Charter of Privileges, more than twenty years ago. The foundries, when they cast bells, always have a text from the Bible to put on them. And what verse do you suppose was chosen to engrave around the edge of the bell that was coming to America? It was as if people knew about today: 'Proclaim Liberty throughout all the land to all the inhabitants thereof.' "

As they gazed up at the tower, the voice of the bell sounded. Slow, dignified, stately, it rang for noon, twelve steady strokes.

The restless moving of the crowd had stopped. All those

men and women were silent. Then came the loud inspiriting roll of drums, like the crackling crash of thunder close at hand. All over the yard the men took off their hats and stood bareheaded. Debby's father and brothers took off their hats. They turned their faces toward the place where the speaker must be standing.

It was thus, standing motionless, gazing up into the blue, blue American sky, that they heard the Declaration of Independence—heard a voice dropping down through the clear bright air, a strong, noble voice slowly, slowly pronouncing the great words one by one, the great words which were to change life for everyone there and for all the nation.

" 'When in the course of human events, it becomes necessary for one people to dissolve the political bands which have connected them with another, and to assume among the powers of the earth, the separate and equal station to which the Laws of Nature and of Nature's God entitle them, a decent respect to the opinions of mankind requires that they should declare the causes which impel them to the separation.

" 'We hold these truths to be self-evident, that all men are created equal, that they are endowed by their Creator with certain unalienable Rights, that among these are Life, Liberty, and the Pursuit of Happiness.' "

The boys lost the thread of what was being said, so shaken were they by the sight of tears in the eyes of the men and women around them and their upturned, shining faces. Slowly, dimly at first, then fast and strong, they felt their own hearts beating. They remembered where they were. They were listening to their nation's voice. And now they heard its words:*

" 'WE, THEREFORE, the Representatives of the UNITED STATES OF AMERICA . . . in the Name, and by Authority of the good People of these Colonies, solemnly publish and declare, That these United Colonies are, and of Right ought to be FREE AND INDEPENDENT STATES: . . . and that as Free and Independent States, they have full Power to levy War, conclude Peace, contract Alliances, establish Commerce, and to do all other Acts and Things which Independent States may of right do. And for the support of this Declaration, with a firm reliance on the protection of Divine Providence, we mutually pledge to each other our Lives, our Fortunes, and our sacred Honor.' "

Those last three words, *"our sacred Honor,"* hung in the silent air. Then such a wild cry of jubilation broke out that for an instant they could not even hear the bell. Could that passionate *clang-clang-clang* be coming from the same bell that had so solemnly struck high noon? The Liberty Bell was ringing in their freedom!

As the shout of the crowd burst forth, the waiting bell-ringers in the other churches, standing by, their hands on the ropes, flung themselves to work and began to pull for dear life. No musical chimes now. Just a joyful, joyful noise which sprang up above the city roofs.

---

*For complete text of the Declaration of Independence see page 141.

The boys were beside themselves with excitement over the noise—the bell, the great bell over their heads, all the bells of the city pealing at once! And everybody was shouting with all his might. With the last of those great words, the crowd had burst into cheering as, with the first tug on its rope, the Liberty Bell had burst into full cry.

The crowd began moving. An outlet to the yard was flung open. Those nearest them poured through it into the street. The pressure inside was lessened. The crowd thinned a little. Still cheering wildly, Debby's family was swept along toward the opening. Stepping fast to keep their feet in the rush, they passed close enough to the State House to catch a glimpse of it through the crowd.

"Oh, look!" cried the boys. A double line of delegates stood in front of the brick wall. They were cheering too. Their voices couldn't be heard above the tumult, but there they stood, those grave serious men, shouting with all their hearts, waving their hats in the air, their faces shining.

The boys tugged at their mother's hands to make her see. "Look! Oh, *look*!" they screamed joyfully to her. "There's Mr. Jefferson! And Mr. *Adams*!"—for John Adams, too—often so grim-faced and once in a while so cross-looking—stout, middle-aged Mr. Adams—was waving his hat wildly in the air and shouting "Hurrah!" his face all brightness.

And Dr. Franklin—he was there too, among the delegates who had come out to hear their Declaration read.

But what was he doing? As they were pushed along through the gate, into the street, they kept turning back to make sure that they really saw what they thought they saw. The stout old man was shouting like everybody else, but he was not just waving his hat. He had put it on the top of his cane, and was spinning it around and around, up high in the air, over everybody's head.

With one final squeeze, the crowd behind them pushed them along out of the gate into the street.

It was packed with people but there was room to breathe. They had shouted till they were panting, and now, wiping their foreheads and breathing deeply, they began to get back to normal.

A man close to them said to their father, as if they were old friends, "Do you know, I could hardly believe it. None of that sounded new to me. It was just what *I* have been wanting to say. If I had known how to put it into words, I would have said just that."

The boys heard their father answer in surprise, "Why, *I* kept thinking that too. It seemed as though I knew it all before."

He shifted Debby to his other shoulder. The boys dropped their mother's hands and walked along behind their parents. Before long, they turned into their street. One of their neighbors, a youngish man, his face working in excitement, came up to their father. "It was the strangest thing!" he cried out. "I thought for a minute that *I* was the person reading that! The words seemed to come from inside my own mind. I've wanted and wanted to say that, only I couldn't quite get it clear in my thoughts."

"Now we all have it clear," answered their father.

Again and again on the way home, the boys heard people saying the same kind of thing. Not till afterward, when people knew the Declaration from reading it in black print on white paper, did they ever hear anybody speak about its being finely written, or having beautiful language like music. On that day, what was felt by those who heard it was that it came from their own hearts and minds.

All the way home they heard pieces of the Declaration floating in the air. Their mother murmured to herself, " 'Life, liberty, and the pursuit of happiness'—I'm so glad they put that last word in! Think of a government set up to help its citizens try to find happiness!"

They were close to their house now. Just ahead of them, their next-door neighbors were turning in at their gate. The two families stood together for a while to talk over the event.

"Did you ever think you'd see this day?" asked Debby's father.

"No, I did not. I can hardly believe it now. I must go right in and write my old grandfather about it. He's ninety-two and his grandfather fought with Cromwell against King Charles the First. He's said right along, old as he is, that we'd have to come to this. He said Cromwell had taught kings they are just men and not gods, and that's what English people would always have to be ready to do."

Then the neighbors went on into their house.

"Let's go sit down a minute under the pear tree," said Debby's mother. "I'm ready to drop."

The boys did drop. On the grass near their parents' chairs.

"Whew!" they said, unbuttoning their collars and taking off their coats.

"Say, Father," said the younger boy, "there was a whole part in the middle that I can't remember at all. I don't seem to have heard it even. I just heard the beginning and the end. What *was* the middle part?"

"It gave the reasons, fifteen years of reasons, for our wanting independence," said his father. "It's going to be printed in the newspapers. It'll be printed in lots of places. You can read it. Probably your schoolmaster will read it to you in school. But you know those reasons, anyhow, or most of them. We all do."

"I'm going to copy it off and learn it by heart," said the older boy, "every word of it."

Part II

The Constitutional Convention
1787

9

Eleven Years Later

Eleven years had passed since the first public reading of
the Declaration of Independence. Mr. Jefferson was now
in Paris, ambassador to France for his new country, the
United States of America; Mr. John Adams was in London, ambassador to England. He was, of course, getting
a very, very cold shoulder from the fine people at the
English Court. The king and his ministers were still running the English government. They naturally hated to
have an *American* ambassador in England. And John
Adams, of all people! The king and his friends had always detested the very name of that Massachusetts man.

Old Dr. Franklin was back in Philadelphia again, living in his own house, just down the street from Debby's
family. He too had been across the ocean for many years,
in France, representing the United States, and was now

more famous than ever. But also much older. He was past eighty now, and his legs that had been so lame during the year when he had gone back and forth from the State House now wouldn't hold him up at all, even with a cane. When he left his home, he had to be carried. Not even in a carriage. That would have been too rough for the old doctor. Any jolt hurt him so much he could hardly bear it. A sort of big box, with a padded chair in it, was arranged for him, with long poles on each side. Every morning his daughter helped get her old father into this, some strong men put their shoulders under leather straps, heaved up, and, walking slowly, carried the ancient philosopher in the first sedan chair Philadelphia had ever seen.

But the fat old gentleman who suffered so much pain and was likely to die any day was as cheerful as ever, and still saw the funny side of things. When he couldn't help it because the pain was so cutting, he groaned out loud. But the next minute he would be cracking a joke.

Somebody cheerful was very much needed just then. For things looked very dismal. The Americans had won the war against Great Britain, yes. But what it had cost them!

The trouble was that they hadn't learned how to stick together. Yet they couldn't succeed as a nation if they didn't.

The trouble with the old way of sticking together, which hadn't worked at all well, was that the agreement had been rushed through while the Americans were at war with England. They couldn't possibly fight the war, each State by itself. So in a great hurry, just because they had to, they had made an agreement to work together. This agreement was called the *Articles of Confederation*.

It hadn't worked well during the war, and it was scarcely working at all now. Yet more than ever the States needed to agree with one another. Everywhere in America, many people were scared to think how helpless their own State would be, by itself, if it were attacked by a big, rich European country with a well-equipped army and navy. And it was not only the great danger from outside. Inside the country there was already a lot of jealousy between the different States. Some of them were beginning to act as though there were no American Confederation left at all, as if they were all separate countries.

If they were separate countries they would have differences of opinion, and every time this happened they would go to war with one another to get their own way. That was the way the European countries had always acted—fighting one another century after century. And look what they had lost in money, deaths, poverty, and misery!

There *must* be some way of getting together that would work better than fighting one another. That's what the convention in 1787 in Philadelphia was to be for: to invent a new set of rules (a Constitution) to create a much-needed central government strong enough to do the things the States desperately needed but could never do by themselves.

Debby was now a slim, long-legged fifteen-year-old girl—as tall as her mother. Hers was a very happy home, full of love and fun; but everything except Debby was worn out and threadbare. Her mother's hair was gray, although she was only forty-six years old. Her father's hair was quite white at fifty. He had to have crutches to walk because his left leg had been cut off. It had been frozen that dreadful winter the American army had spent at Valley Forge. The soldiers had had mighty little to eat and, despite the deep snow on the ground, most of them had worn ragged old coats and scarcely any shoes at all. The soldiers' feet had been bruised and bleeding. Yet their country was not so poor that it could not buy shoes for its own soldiers. The reason was a legal one. The *Articles of Confederation*—that first set of hastily invented rules—didn't provide any way for the Continental Congress to get taxes which would have brought in enough money from the States to buy new clothes and shoes and decent food for the American soldiers.

So Debby's father lost a leg for lack of the right kind of Constitution. He had a job now in the post office. It was work at a desk, work a veteran could do even with one leg gone. The family had breakfast early so that he would have time to hobble downtown on his crutches.

He received a salary, of course. But it was paid by the United States government. So his pay was in paper money. "Continental Currency" it was called, and it was worth just exactly nothing. Or almost. The Continental Congress hadn't had any legal power to make the States pay their fair share of the nation's expenses. Then, too, during the war there was so much confusion and uncertainty, and the States were so poor, that most of them paid very little. So the Continental Congress had to go on printing paper money. The more they printed, the less it would buy. People with things to sell were afraid it would be worth even less tomorrow than today. So, to be on the safe side, they raised the prices of food and clothing.

If it hadn't been for the two boys, Debby's family would scarcely have been able to manage at all. They were grown-up men of twenty-five and twenty-three now. The older one, like his father, had been in the American army, and one winter had camped out in Chester County, not far from Philadelphia. There he had met a farmer's family, and after the American victory had married the farmer's daughter. They had a little boy now. So Debby had become "Aunt Deborah."

The farm was a fine one, on rich, deep, fertile soil. Americans were lucky in those hard days if somebody in the family lived on a farm. Every so often the Chester County family would hitch their two horses to the farm wagon and drive in to visit the folks in Philadelphia. They always brought presents from the farm. Sometimes it was a couple of fleeces from their sheep. Out of this wool Debby and her mother made homespun cloth for their menfolks' coats and breeches and their own winter

dresses. Or they knitted stockings and coats and underwear and even winter nightgowns and nightcaps. Or
they used that homespun thread for the endless darning
and mending. Everything in the house was wearing out—
rugs, wraps, underwear.

As for food, they used every inch of their back garden
to grow vegetables. Now the pear tree stood in the middle of a small field, where peas and beans and squash
and pumpkins and corn grew right up to the back door.
Debby and her mother worked there, with her father, to
raise food. Everybody on their street was raising food like
this. The younger people couldn't remember when they
didn't.

They went without a good many things, including
anything new for the house. No, there *was* one new
thing. A big framed picture of General George Washington. This hung over the mantelpiece. Debby couldn't
remember when it had not hung there. But one day
when she was cleaning the attic her older brother was
with her. He found a framed picture, face down, under
the eaves. Debby had never noticed it before. He pulled
it out, stood it up, wiped off some of the dust, and gazed
at it a long time.

"Who is that?" asked Debby, looking over his shoulder. "A man with a fat face like that shouldn't wear such
a high collar."

Her brother was astonished. "Don't you *know*?" he
cried out.

She looked again. "No. Should I?"

Her brother saw that she really didn't recognize the face. "Well, you *are* an American girl!" he exclaimed. "That's King George III. It used to hang in our living room, just where George Washington's picture is now. Think of your not even remembering!"

"Oh, I was only four years old," said Debby. "How could I?"

She went on sweeping while her brother set the picture up and gazed at it. "It takes me back," he murmured. "I remember so well the day when Mother took it down." To his sister he said, "Do you know, our brother told me that the last time his ship was in an English port—Bristol, I think it was—everybody there was gossiping about the king's going crazy. Really crazy, you know. Insane. People were saying he'd soon have to be locked up, or put into a strait jacket, to keep him from attacking the people around him."

Debby had no comment to make on this. She did not care a bit what happened to a king. Why should she? She was an American.

Her brother was still gazing at the picture. He said thoughtfully, "Maybe he was sort of crazy all the time? None of us ever thought of that."

Debby reached with her broom for a spider web on the slanting rafters.

"I suppose," meditated her brother, "that a person *is* crazy who gets so mad if every single person doesn't agree right off with every single thing he says."

Debby didn't pay much attention. She was more interested when people discussed the possibility of getting a new Constitution that would be better than the agreement the States had hastily scrambled together in wartime. Debby saw the need for that. Anybody with an eye in her head understood that if the States could really act together and support a central government, it would mean something. If they got some rules made about taxes paid to the government that would give her father his salary in good hard money—that would not be "history," that would be news.

They were all proud that Philadelphia was the place where this important convention would be held. Yet her mother would not consider taking in one of the delegates as roomer or boarder. Other families around them did. There was an extra room in the house, the one the boys had had. But her mother shook her head.

"I don't mind living as poorly as we do," she said. "I'm proud of the reason for it—that we are now free people in a free country—and I don't grudge what it cost. Not even your dear father's leg, not my gray hairs. But I can't bear to have a stranger from another State, where maybe they do have money to buy new things, come into this house and see everything patched and darned, even the sheets on the bed. And have nothing to eat but fried Indian-corn mush and scrapple."

"Oh, I love fried mush and scrapple!" exclaimed Debby.

"You poor child! You can't even remember what a

good meal is like—when we used to have roast leg of lamb, and fried chicken, and jellies and custards whenever we wanted them. I'm not complaining! I count it a privilege to have given something up for independence. But all the same, I don't want strangers in here—maybe rich strangers—to see our rags.

"It's not our clothes I mind so much, although I sometimes wonder what my mother would have thought to see my petticoats nothing but patches on patches. But housekeeping gear—she brought me up to keep a house in good condition. I haven't anything left to patch the towels *with*! And the covering on our chairs is so ragged that it won't take any more darning."

So one day in late May 1787, when Debby went to the front door to answer a knock on it, and a strange man asked to see her mother about renting a room for the duration of the Constitutional Convention, Debby knew what her mother's answer would be.

But she went to get her and then sat down in a corner of the living room to hear what was said.

To her, the visitor looked like anybody else. He was a little younger than her father, but his hair was grizzled; he was dressed in gray woolen clothes, his shoes were of stout black leather with steel buckles, now rather dusty. He kept his left hand in his pocket.

"I've been trying everywhere, madam," he said, "to find a room within my means. My expenses here are paid in Continental money, of course. It's only fair to let you know that, to begin with. And I haven't any hard money of my own to spare. My business went down a great deal during the war. I was sorry to have to leave it now, just when it is beginning to look up a little. At least, I hoped it was. A man hardly knows *how* to run his business, with such uncertainty about our money. I have a family, my wife and three boys. And a baby girl born since the war. Like most people, we barely make both ends meet. We live very plainly. But my wife and I do not grudge the price. My wife has been a patriot from the beginning."

He went on, "I need only a bed, breakfast, and supper. The main meal I plan to take with other delegates at the Indian Queen Hotel. Several of the wealthier delegates are living there, but that's beyond my means, and the management of the hotel has arranged for a private dining room for those who wish to eat together after sessions of the convention. I believe I can afford that."

He paused for the answer of Debby's mother. It wasn't an answer yet. It was a question. "Were you—did you serve in the war?" she asked.

"Yes, I enlisted among the first, I am proud to say. That is how I lost this hand." He lifted his left arm and showed a scarred stump.

"Oh!" said Debby's mother softly. "In which battle?" she asked respectfully.

"Not in battle at all," he said. "It was frozen, that winter in Valley Forge. The army doctors had to cut it off."

Debby's mother stood up and made the visitor a deep curtsy. "We will be glad to have you room with us," she said.

He stood up too. And now Debby could see that, for all his simple clothes and quiet manner, he had a distinguished look about him.

"Thank you very much," he said with a bow. But he was still uneasy. "I hope the price—" he began. "I want to make it clear I have only Continental money."

"We will be glad to accept any American money," said Debby's mother grandly, "till a new Constitution provides better." She said earnestly to him, "Sir, my husband lost his leg at Valley Forge. You are welcome in this American home."

10

Hard Work Ahead

Debby's father agreed at once to the new plan. He was especially pleased when he heard that the delegate had been in Valley Forge during that terrible winter which had cost him his leg. The two men did not seem—at least to Debby and her mother—to talk together much about this, or about anything. But they evidently enjoyed each other's company nonetheless, in the few hours they were together, smoking their pipes in a comfortable, friendly silence broken by an occasional brief remark.

They were both tired when evening came; Debby's father from his slow, tiresome trip to and from his desk at the post office, the delegate from the long, steady sessions of the convention. The regular meetings began at ten or eleven in the morning and lasted without any recess till four or sometimes five in the afternoon. And often enough, work on special committees had to be done earlier or later than that. It made a long, hard day.

Perhaps the delegate (Debby and her mother soon spoke of him as "Our Delegate") was glad to be with another tired man who expected nothing from him but sociable silence while they waited for the evening meal to be put on the table. Perhaps he was relieved to be in a house where the family did not attempt to persuade him to break the promise, given by all the members of the convention, not to tell anybody anything about the matters they argued over day after day.

The Continental Congress—the one which had put out the Declaration of Independence—had also agreed not to tell outsiders about their debates. But that had been a very different kind of meeting. They had constantly needed news from the outside, from the different colonies which were, one by one, turning themselves into American States. Express riders had always been coming and going to the State House, their heavy, spurred riding boots showing the mud or snow or dust from far distant parts of the country. Nobody knew what was in their mailbags, but newspaper readers knew what was going on at Charleston, or Hartford, or with the army. So with their newspapers and their gossip, and with public proclamation from time to time, Philadelphia people had always been able to piece together some notion of what the Continental Congress must be talking about inside the State House.

But this convention was different. The delegates

needed no more information from the outside than what they had all brought with them to Philadelphia. They knew—everybody did—that things were not going well, that the country was in mortal danger. The American States were falling apart—in spite of the wounds and deaths and heartbreaking sorrow with which independence had been won. These sober-faced men from almost all the States who now walked the streets of Philadelphia did not risk being hanged as traitors if they failed. Yet if they failed, the Liberty Bell would have rung in vain.

If they failed, their country would fail. The Revolutionary War was over and won. But now they had to fight a harder battle. Now they were assembled not to fight a war against another country, but to win a victory over that side of human nature which makes everyone want his own way so much that he comes to believe his way is the only right way.

The thirteen States, from New Hampshire to Georgia, needed one another. They knew perfectly well that they were not strong enough to stand alone. That is why they all (except Rhode Island, which was sulking) sent delegates to this Constitutional Convention. But could their delegates keep their heads and not get angry when they saw that no one of them could have everything he wanted?

That was the question before the delegates who, on a rainy day, May 25th, 1787, walked or rode to the State House and met in the very same hall where the Declaration of Independence had been signed. All over America, people were hoping and praying that the delegates would succeed, because if they did, America could leap forward to be strong, prosperous, safe, happy.

All over Europe, kings and princes and prime ministers hoped they would fail, because that would prove what the rulers of those times wanted proved: that ordinary people aren't smart enough to run their own government, but must have a king or dictator to give them orders.

No wonder that Our Delegate looked very serious as he started off through the rain to the first meeting.

As far as Debby's family was concerned, he walked away from the house into another world. He was an honorable man, and they were mannerly people who wouldn't dream of coaxing him to break his promise. So each morning Debby handed her delegate his hat, held his overcoat for him to put on, and watched him walk away from the house. That was all. She knew nothing of what he did till he came back that afternoon, walking slowly, and glad to drop into a chair and silently smoke a pipe with her father.

Many, many years after this all-important convention, when nearly every member had died, it was considered safe to publish the records of its work, day by day, speech by speech, debate by debate. Mr. James Madison of Virginia, one of the delegates, had taken down in a kind of shorthand what had happened, and fifty years after the end of the convention, the American Congress in Washington, D.C., had this record printed in three volumes. These volumes are still available today in many large libraries.

That is how readers nowadays can find out much more about the day-by-day activities of the convention than Philadelphians knew while it was going on.

In a chair on a low platform, in front of the delegates' seats, sat General George Washington, who was president of this convention. He was big-nosed, broad-shouldered, tall, and ruddy-faced, just as he had been eleven years before. But then he was only a Virginia Colonel of Militia. Now he had been Commander in Chief of the American armies all through those long, struggling, hoping, fearing, despairing, and hoping again years of the War for Independence. Now he was one of the world's famous men.

In the United States he was famous because he had been the head general of the army and had, in the end, with the help of France, won independence for the new nation. In England and the rest of Europe he was famous because, when the war was over, he had thankfully taken off his uniform and gone back to farming. Most people outside America had expected him to use his fame and success, and the fact that the army had the habit of taking orders from him, to make himself king of America.

And while some of the Europeans admired Washington for his astonishing (to them) idea of passing up the chance to grab and hold on to power, still they wondered whether he hadn't made a mistake. They thought that if *he* wasn't king, somebody else would have to be. Perhaps someone not so good as Washington.

What such people outside of America were saying to themselves went something like this: The Articles of Confederation had worked only after a poor fashion, even when the new American States had been forced to stick together or get beaten in the war. Even then the American army hadn't been paid regularly (often not at all) or well fed, or decently clothed. And now that the war was over, the so-called central "government" was cracking at the seams and breaking up into little pieces—into thirteen little pieces, not one of them amounting to anything. "You just watch and see what a failure they'll make of this Constitutional Convention!" they said. "Trying to patch up their old Confederation, are they? They won't make it any better. Can't be done—not without lords and dukes and a king and so forth and so on." That's what a lot of people outside of America thought and believed. And how they hoped they were right!

Just the opposite was hoped by the delegates as they gathered that first morning and looked up at George Washington in the president's chair. No one would have known from anything he did that he was one of the world's famous men. He never had been much of a talker, and now he had lost his own teeth and had artificial ones carved out of ivory. They were the best any dentist in those days knew how to make but they fitted his mouth so badly that talking was hard for him.

Some of the delegates had been members of the Continental Congress which had voted the Declaration of Independence, so they knew General Washington by sight. But for some of them this was the first time they had ever laid eyes on him, though his picture hung in nearly every American home. They gave this famous man a good long look.

There he sat, tall, broad, blue-eyed, fifty-five years old, without much expression except a look on his face that showed he would never stop trying to do whatever ought to be done. He wasn't often lively or gay. But according to the records he seldom looked anxious or uncertain, although we know from his letters that he was often as worried as anybody else there, and as much afraid that they wouldn't make a go of it.

There was one other very famous man inside that hall. In one of the delegates' chairs sat Dr. Franklin. Sometimes he dozed off in a catnap. But he never lost the thread of the discussions and was always ready to open his eyes to say something spicy, wise, or funny. For he was naturally just as lively as George Washington was quiet. His broad, wrinkled old face was bright with interest in everything that went on, but it didn't show, any more than Washington's, what he was really feeling. For he too was terribly anxious for fear they might not make a go of putting together a set of rules that would really work.

For ten years he had been in France, representing America. He knew how much the great and rich and powerful people over there hoped and prayed that this convention would turn out badly, and thus prove what they wanted proved—that everyday folks never know enough to run a country. Dr. Franklin knew, too, how the everyday people of Europe, and the generous-hearted ones, whether they were ordinary or great folks, hoped and prayed for the new nation's success. All this weighed heavily on him. He was well past eighty and not very well. He knew he hadn't long to live. But his quick, alert eyes watched everything, sizing up each delegate as somebody who'd help or harm this great effort to step forward from the past and what governments always had done, to the future and what they might do.

11

Let's Make a Fresh Start

The delegates settled down to work at the State House. They were friendly and busy, and got along faster than expected. This was because the seven Virginia delegates had done a lot of thinking in advance, had written out a plan for a new Constitution, and had it all ready for discussion.

Governor Randolph of Virginia made a speech explaining the plan and what was wrong with the old government. It took him quite a while, and most of what he said was familiar to the delegates because they knew before they got to Philadelphia that there was plenty wrong with the Articles of Confederation. But they listened with patient attention, hour after hour. They hadn't come to the Constitutional Convention to be amused, but to save their country, so they listened carefully to every word.

Governor Randolph pointed out that under the Confederation the idea was that the States were independent (or "sovereign," as they called themselves). That meant that each State thought it could do just as it pleased. The agreement that joined them stated that they would act together only as much and when and as long as they pleased. This plan had not worked well, as they all knew, and according to Governor Randolph it never would work well because:

It didn't give them enough security, since none of the States could be *sure* of help from the others if it should be attacked by England or Spain or any other powerful foreign country.

Also, there were a good many things needed in the new nation—needed not by one but by all the States—such as opening rivers up for ships, building canals for carrying goods and passengers, building good roads from State to State for getting the mail carried, a national army kept in good shape to help put down riots and rebellions too serious for the local State Militia to handle. These and other much-needed things would cost much more than any one State had money for. But if they all put in their share, the money could easily be raised.

In addition, the central government ought to be able to crack down on any State which made laws hurting another, as New York was doing by charging a tariff on anything brought in for sale from New Jersey and Connecticut.

And so on and so forth. It was as plain as anything

could be that the old Confederation couldn't be put together into any new Constitution that would work. What they would have to put together was a brand-new plan, with the States managing their own private affairs inside their own boundaries, but outside of them working with all the other States under rules they would all agree on. A central government would have to be set up, elected by the people of all the States.. This central government would make laws to take care of things needed by the whole country—and it would need power enough to get those laws obeyed. AND, of course, since it couldn't get its work done without money, it would have to have the right to raise the money it needed by taxes. The old Confederation had had no way to pay its bills, except by promises that the bills would be paid sometime in the future if somehow the Confederation could get hold of a little real money. Unfortunately, Continental money wasn't worth much.

Up to this time the delegates had thought of their States as independent countries, free at all times to decide what they would or wouldn't do. They hadn't yet faced the fact that nobody in the world can be free to do just what he pleases, any time he feels like it. If he does, he'll interfere with other people and they will fight back. The State legislatures had sent their delegates to Philadelphia thinking that they could tighten up the bearings and put new oil and grease into the wheezy old Confederation machine and get it going. This plan for a new, superior, strong national government went far beyond what they had expected.

Still, all of them had learned the hard way that you can't do business, or run a government—you can't even pay your household bills—with money that tomorrow will buy fewer groceries, or overalls, or bricks and hardware than it will today. Many of them had been almost starved and frozen in the Revolutionary Army. They knew Congress hadn't held back uniforms and rations just to be mean. It failed to supply food and shoes for the soldiers because it didn't have the money to buy them. Even during the Revolutionary War, the States had never paid in their full share to the general treasury. So the delegates decided that a national Congress would just have to be given the right to tax—and to issue sound money worth its face value.

But money wouldn't settle everything. There would need to be general laws which *everybody* had to follow. These men had experience. They knew a lot about how to run a business or a government, or they wouldn't have been chosen as delegates. They had sense enough to know that, separately, no single State would ever amount to much. But if the thirteen of them could agree, the new nation had a good chance of being successful.

Plenty of the delegates were worried about one part of the plan or another. They had fought so hard against the power of England to give them orders that they were fearful of the power that was to be given to the new central government by the new plan.

But finally they voted to start fresh, and invent a new government with a new Constitution.

While the delegates were arguing, Debby's family was bursting with curiosity. They never asked direct questions. But they did watch their delegate closely when he came back for supper. They tried to guess by his manner how convention business was going. Pretty well, they thought at first—at least as well as could be expected. Some nights he seemed tired from listening to long speeches, and he always looked serious from carrying a great responsibility, but at least for some weeks he seemed quite easy in his mind. His appetite was good. He told them about his wife and his little red-haired, postwar daughter, "the first American-born in our home," as he said. He was interested in the garden.

"We'll have peas for supper before long," said Debby's mother, "and maybe the Indian corn will be ripe before you go home." Then she worried for fear he might think she was trying to draw from him an opinion as to how long the convention would last. It was really hard *always* to remember that he had promised not to tell anybody a single thing about what he did all day.

Debby thought it was nonsense. "What's the use of being so secret?" she asked.

Her father thought a while, then finally answered. "I suppose the idea of this convention is to talk over all the possible plans for government and finally pick out the one that promises best. The delegates are here to put their heads together and talk reasonably and listen to reason. It might be easier for them to be convinced by somebody else's good ideas and change their own if the people back home don't know how their delegates vote. But that is only my guess. I really don't know."

12

Roses for Debby

All through those early weeks the family's delegate looked calm and untroubled in spite of his load of responsibility, as if he felt that somehow or other everything would work out all right. Once he even said so. Debby's father had been telling him that it was only because of the hard times that they had to use all their backyard to grow food. He said that before the war they had had a pleasant strip of grass near the house, and some benches under the pear tree where they often sat on a summer evening.

"You will again," said the delegate heartily. "When our convention has finished its labor, our nation's affairs will be in order as they have never been before. Our debts will be paid. A good taxation system will bring in a reasonable revenue to our national government. We can expect our commerce to grow greatly. Our shipping will need to grow as much. Your son will be a ship's captain. Your salary, sir, will be paid in gold coins, if you would like it so. And Miss Debby here can have India-lawn dresses, all printed over with posies."

That was good news.

But about the middle of June, their guest stopped being cheerful. He came back to the house dragging his feet. He was always mannerly and never gruff, but he grew more and more silent. He was thinking hard about something. It was something so troubling, judging from his worried face, that he hardly heard what they said to him, hardly saw what was around him in the house, in the vegetable garden, on his plate.

His appetite left him too. It was the time of year when, in the Philadelphia climate, the strawberries are ripe, the green peas are meltingly delicious, the asparagus and the rhubarb are still tender and savory. The son's family on the fine farm in Chester County felt, as everybody else did, that they wanted to do their share to honor a delegate to the meeting from which so much was hoped by the whole nation, so they sent or brought in young broilers, fresh eggs, rashers of bacon, hams, a guinea hen once in a while. Deborah had never eaten so well in her life. But their guest picked forlornly at this delicious food "like a sick child," mourned Debby's mother. He ate a little, and then sat, his knife and fork in his hand, staring at nothing.

They were all deeply troubled. For there could be no reason for his low spirits except that the convention was not going well.

Toward the end of June their delegate addressed himself to Debby's mother one evening. "Madam," he said, "I trust what I am about to ask will not seem improper to you. My sleeping is poor these nights. In fact, I am barely sleeping at all. I have thought that perhaps if I could sometimes, without disturbing your household, arise and walk up and down the path in your garden it might allay my restlessness."

Debby's mother begged him to do anything that might be of help to him.

Debby's father said, after hesitating a little, "Sir, my nights too are not good. Would it be presuming if sometimes I joined you there?"

The delegate took his host's hand in his. "It will comfort me, my friend, to have a veteran from Valley Forge with me."

So, during the hot first part of July, Debby and her mother often heard the stairs creak as their guest went down in his stocking feet. He would pause a moment silently at the door of the downstairs bedroom where Debby's father slept, and then go out to sit on the threshold of the back door to put his shoes on. Then, often, there was the familiar thump of the crutch in the hall— and out into the darkness went the two veterans to pace slowly up and down the garden path on the soft open ground, between the rows of Indian corn.

Although Debby's mother didn't walk the floor those nights, she too did not sleep well. She lay in her bed, her eyes wide open in the blackness, her heart heavy, her mind full of fears.

She had a cousin about her age whose husband worked as clerk in the State House, but not for the convention. Sometimes, when he had a great deal of work, he would go back to his desk in the evening to finish it. Debby's mother had never told her cousin anything about the sleepless night wanderings of their delegate. She did not tell anybody, and made Debby promise not to mention it. "It might make people fear that things are not going well with the making of the new Constitution," she said. "Since we have a delegate in our house, we must take our share of his promise of not letting people know anything about their proceedings."

But she herself found it hard not to show her alarm at something her cousin told her about this time. "Do you suppose," said her cousin, "that they are having trouble getting together on the Constitution in the convention?"

"What makes you think that?" asked Debby's mother quickly, looking and feeling as anxious as she had been when her husband was in the Continental Army, half starved, half frozen, without enough powder and shot for his musket.

Her cousin went on, "Well, I wouldn't speak of it to anybody but you, but this is what my husband told me. Last night he was working at his desk in the State House and happened to look out of the window. He saw that somebody was inside the walls of the yard. You know nobody is supposed to go in there now, during the time the convention is meeting. The armed sentries have orders to keep everybody out. My husband went down to call one of the sentries. But he didn't. For who do you suppose it was, walking up and down there in the twilight? General Washington! General George Washington. All by himself. Walking up and down, up and down the path, his hands behind his back. All alone. It was getting darker. He didn't notice. He just walked up and down, up and down—"

The two women looked at each other in heartbroken alarm. Was their new nation already in trouble?

But then—what a relief! One evening the delegate actually cleaned up his plate at supper, and told them how much he had enjoyed the tender young string beans. Their spirits soared. Things must be going more smoothly at the Constitutional Convention.

Their spirits soared higher still on the 13th when he came into the house, a broad smile on his face, bringing a bouquet of roses for the table. He said he had overheard them remarking that July 13th was Debby's birthday.

They were happy that evening, although they had no idea what had happened. They were proud, too, over a compliment to their State paid by their guest as he sat with Debby's father.

"Very fine men you have in Pennsylvania," he said.

"You have reason to be proud of them."

Debby's mother answered, "Yes, Dr. Franklin is indeed a great sage and a famous philosopher."

"I am sure he is," said their guest, "but I was speaking of your Mr. Wilson." He drew a long pull on his pipe, took it out of his mouth, looked up at the ceiling as though he were trying to think of the right words, and said warmly and emphatically, "Mr. Wilson is an honor to the human race."

Debby stared, not knowing the name. Her mother quickly gave her a Philadelphia kind of explanation. "He's a cousin of Molly Cutler's mother."

And that was all Debby knew—until she was much older.

But Mr. Madison's report of the meetings, published years later, explains exactly what happened to the Congress and the delegates on and before that July 13th.

The first days of the convention had been full of pleasant good will. "The Virginia plan," presented by Governor Randolph, had been carefully put together with detailed clauses and subheadings, all thought out to take care of anything that might happen to a government—with judges and courts, and representatives in a legislature, and everything else provided for. The other delegates hadn't anything prepared, and for the first weeks they all sailed forward on general ideas.

Then they had run smack into a very big problem. Some States were large and had lots of people in them.

107

Other States were small. Suddenly everything came to a halt. The delegates were hung up on a difference of opinion which couldn't ever—so far as they could see—be settled, because the problem would never change. There would always be large States and small ones. And people had grown so used to the idea of States that it seemed against nature to admit that some of them were less important than others. How could any government be devised which would be fair both to the small States, such as Delaware and New Jersey, and to the big States, such as Massachusetts and Pennsylvania?

There was to be a national legislature, of course. No argument. For many years they had all grown used to that way of government in their own States. But should the national lawmakers be elected by the State legislatures? A few delegates thought so, but they didn't put up much of a fight. It was settled that the people should vote directly for one part of the national legislature (the one now called the House of Representatives).

How many of these representatives should each State send? That was a hard question. If every forty thousand people elected one representative, that would mean only one or two apiece for each of the smaller States. They didn't like the idea. Under that plan a couple of the bigger States could outvote all the smaller ones. Delaware and New Jersey representatives might as well stay home, for all the influence they would have.

The big States came right back with the question, "Is it fairer to vote the way we now do in the Continental

Congress—and right here in the convention—one vote to each State, large or small? That means that a few people in seven small or medium States can determine the fate of a lot more people in the other six States."

In general, as far as the logic of the argument went, the large States had the best of it, so the delegates from the little States threatened that if they couldn't have their way they'd go back home. Such a threat was tragically serious. For it would be very dangerous to have some of the States standing out from the Union. Dangerous to the solitary State, and even more dangerous to the whole country.

The danger of a failure to get all the States into one nation finally erupted in red-hot angry words when one of the delegates from Delaware said furiously that his State would never, never submit to the larger ones. Had they fought and suffered in the War for Independence only to fall under the tyranny of their neighbors? He was so excited that he went on to threaten that if Delaware did stay out of the Union she might make a bargain with a foreign country and become part of some nation from across the Atlantic, which would give her a better deal than her fellow Americans.

In that company of men who had fought so wildly to get out of the power of a nation from across the Atlantic, this threat of having such a nation established in their midst was horrifying.

The delegates kept at it hammer and tongs for days. Something had to be done.

And something was done.

To the eternal credit of the Constitutional Convention, although all the members wanted their own way, they wanted still more to set up the best possible government for their country. So what they did was to appoint a committee, one member from each State, to see if they couldn't find *some* sort of a plan everyone could agree to. Just after the 4th of July, this committee brought in its report: In the House of Representatives there should be one representative for every forty thousand people; that gave the larger States the most power there. But in the national Senate every State should have an equal vote, the small States just the same as the big ones.

This is called the *Federal Compromise*. To the present day, this is the way the United States government works.

Nobody was altogether satisfied with this solution. It was rather like cutting up the apple and giving everyone a slice. But at first, at least, the idea seemed to have broken a hole through the solid wall that had threatened to halt all progress. It pointed the way toward a union everyone could agree to.

Those were the days when Debby's delegate began to feel better, and stopped walking in the garden most of the night. Maybe the new plan wasn't the very best one imaginable, but it might work, if everyone gave it a fair chance.

But then one morning a delegate got up and introduced a totally different idea. "Money is power," he said. "Wealth ought to count just as much as the number of voters in a government which, like all governments, really is formed for the protection of property, since government is supported by property."

Another delegate pointed out that a lot of poor people were moving over the mountains into western lands. Before long there might be more votes there than in the rich, old, settled, original thirteen States along the seacoast. *That* couldn't be allowed!

And then, before the delegates had had time to discuss the question thoroughly, it was voted that for all new States, representation in Congress should be figured partly on the number of voters and partly on *how much money they represented.*

Those were bad days and nights for the family's delegate. At first he was so discouraged that he didn't even try to get up and walk in the garden. He just lay awake in his bed and worried. Protection of property was all right. No one would work hard and be thrifty unless the law protected his savings. And it was true enough that a rich man, just because he was rich and could hire and fire men working for him, always had more power than a poor man. But that didn't prove that the law ought to be rigged to give him more power still. Nor did it mean that he was any better as a citizen than an honest, brainy man who hadn't so much money.

It got so bad that on the night of July 12th, just before Debby's birthday, the delegate dragged himself out of bed again. Step by step, to and fro on the garden path he

walked, trying to figure it out. Was it all worthwhile, he
asked himself. Was it to set money ahead of human beings that his host had lost his leg? Had he been fighting
in the American army, not for his country as he had
thought, but to make money powerful? Was it just to
safeguard money that in the Declaration of Independence
the Americans had all pledged—through their representatives—"our lives, our fortunes and our sacred honor"?
"Honor" is a great word, he thought, plodding to and fro
on the earth of that path. Did I then promise by my
sacred honor that I would do my best to keep rich men in
power in our government?

Perhaps other delegates agreed with the idea. They
seemed to. Nobody protested. Perhaps he was the only
person in the convention who did not like this idea of
pulling off your hat to money rather than to character,
honesty, and good sense. His fellow delegates seemed by
their silence to take it for granted that if a man had
money, it proved he had more character and honesty and
good will and intelligence than a man who hadn't.

Next morning the delegate was worn out after that
sleepless night. He ate his hominy and bacon and corn
bread and molasses for breakfast, but his mind was full
of anxiety. Very dimly he heard somebody at the table
say that this was the birthday of the young daughter of
his hosts. But his own mind was filled with despondent
thoughts.

He walked to the State House and slumped into his
chair. Then things began to happen. First Mr. Randolph,

a rich man from Virginia, the governor of that State, made a surprising motion. He moved to strike out the word "wealth" in the rules for giving representatives to new States.

Mr. Wilson of Pennsylvania stood up to speak next. It was a long, brilliant, unforgettable speech. What it amounted to in plain words was this: All men wherever they live have equal rights. We need not be troubled by the fear that someday the "Interior Country" might have more votes than the old States. If they come to have the most votes, then they will deserve to run the government. We must not forget that England tried to keep America from growing too strong—and as a result the British forced us to fight and to win our freedom. We of the old States must not make the same mistake with our western settlers. And as for the argument that "wealth must rule"—here his voice rang out clear and strong— he didn't believe a word of it. "Property is NOT the chief object of government and society," he said. "Society's chief and most noble purpose is the cultivation of the human mind." Therefore he hoped others would join him in supporting Mr. Randolph's motion.

Mr. Wilson, the great Pennsylvania lawyer, so respected for his brains and his education, was talking exactly the way that Thomas Jefferson had written: "We hold these truths to be self-evident." But would the other delegates agree?

General Washington quietly put the question: "All in favor of Mr. Randolph's motion will say 'Aye.' "

Every State represented, except one, voted to leave out the word "wealth." During all the meetings of the convention, there was scarcely another vote on which they were so united. In their hearts they had *all* been thinking alike. Even those who had spoken in favor of wealth being as important as human beings had been carried along.

That afternoon, when his usual late meal with the other members of the convention was finished, the family's delegate felt so happy, so relieved that he couldn't just walk back into the house and sit down in a chair. He was full of new hope and energy! He would have to use up some of it before he could be quiet. Strange to be restless now because he was so happy!

He struck out at random, up one street and down another, wherever his feet took him. " 'Property is *not*,' " he said aloud, quoting from Mr. Wilson's speech, " 'the sole or primary object of government and society.' "

He walked faster, made a wide sweep with his arm. "The most noble object is the cultivation and improvement of the human mind," he said earnestly to a sycamore tree. "We are founding our country's government not to give men a chance to get rich, but to live, be free, find out *how to be happy.*"

" 'Life, liberty, and the pursuit of happiness,' " he exclaimed to the nearest lamppost. He forgot his usual care to keep the ugly scarred stump of his left arm out of sight in his pocket. He was proud of it and what it meant, for it *had* been worthwhile, after all, to have fought the War for Independence.

People glanced back at him as they passed—a sober, middle-aged, quietly dressed man, yet talking to himself as he went along the street, his face shining with joy.

Presently he slowed down his swinging pace. He had come into the flower market. As he looked at the summer roses, he remembered dimly—didn't somebody speak of today's being a birthday? Whose could it be? Oh, yes, the young girl at his boardinghouse. "Give me that bunch of roses, will you please?" he said to the woman at the stand, and reached into his coat for his pocketbook.

13

Another Hill to Climb

A few days later, on July 16, the members of the Constitutional Convention were disagreeing again. This time
it wasn't the question of a State's having more votes if it
had more money. Mr. Wilson had killed that idea for
good. It was the old argument over one vote to each State
in the Senate. Virginia, Pennsylvania, and South Carolina made one last try to upset that. They couldn't quite
do it, so the Federal Compromise still stood, but when
the rumpus was over, that part of the plan had a majority
of only a single vote. Everybody began to feel, "Oh, what's
the use? We'll never get our plan adopted by the States
if we are so divided ourselves about it."

It is important to remember that by their voting these
delegates had no power to bind anyone except each other.
The States themselves had the final say-so. When the

Constitution was finished, it would have to be voted on by conventions in each of the thirteen States. If nine of these States liked it, the new government would be established, in the hope that the other four would come in later. Unless nine States were willing to try it, nothing would happen.

No wonder they were dismal that day when they found they were still almost half-and-half divided on one of their most important ideas. After working all summer, talking, thinking, explaining, if they hadn't gotten any closer together than that, what chance would their Constitution stand in the State conventions? Not much, they thought. Many delegates felt they might as well give up and go home. A few of them said so out loud.

But they didn't go home. They weren't the sort to quit. And the first thing they knew, they were over the hump.

It happened this way. The very next morning, before time for the meeting to begin, delegates from the big States came to the Assembly Hall and sat around the president's table to talk things over. They were all absolutely frank. This idea of one vote in the Senate to each State—no matter how small—is not fair, they said. Nothing could make them think differently. But, after all, it had been voted. Then one of the delegates said, "Even though we can't do what we think best, we ought to stick around and do the best we can. That's what we're here for." He was saying out loud what most of them were already thinking.

By this time a good many delegates from the smaller

States had come into the hall and were standing near the table, listening. "It sounds as if these delegates from the big States are trying to be fair," they commented among themselves. "They aren't planning to gang up on us and push us around. And they're right about not quitting. We're here to do the best we can, even if our best isn't perfect. They say they don't like everything in the proposed Constitution. Well, *we* don't either! But if we all work together and keep at it, we can certainly turn in a plan of government a lot better than the Articles of Confederation. We've got to."

From that day on the going was better. There were still plenty of rough spots, plenty of disagreements, plenty of sharp words during debate, but no one doubted any longer that some sort of a Constitution was going to be worked out.

What did they disagree about? About almost every idea that came up. For one thing, about having a president. Everyone knew that someone had to be in charge to see that laws were carried out, to make sure that money was honestly and carefully spent, and in general to act as the chief and head of the government. But would it be wise to trust all that power to one man? Maybe a committee of three would be safer. The same old fear was worrying them. A single president might sooner or later get all the power into his own hands and make himself king. But three men could watch one another. Some of the delegates said foolish things about Caesar and Oliver Cromwell and the "tyrants of ancient Greece," but fortunately most of the members of the convention kept their wits about them. They pointed out that a board of three governors would be continually ducking responsibility or shifting it around. Nothing would get decided. A single boss can make up his mind and stick to it.

So the new nation got a single president, and now, after two hundred years, Americans still live under a republic, not a despotism.

There were plenty of other questions still to be worked out. Who was to elect this president? Should he be elected by Congress? Or by the State legislatures? Or by all the citizens in a general election? The convention had to decide which method to choose.

And law courts—some agreement had to be reached about those. Each State had its own law courts. But how about disputes growing out of the national laws Congress was going to make? Shouldn't there be some sort of national law court to settle these? The new Constitution did provide for such a national law court, and this was the start of the Supreme Court.

Then came the question of treaties with foreign countries. Who would have the power to make those? And tax money? How much of the money raised by taxes should be granted to the central government? How much should be left to the States? And so on and so on. It would be impossible to try to cover here all the questions that arose and how each one was settled.

*   *   *

The important fact to remember is that the Founding Fathers knew that, in the Constitution they were writing, they would have to make sure that no group of officials, and no single person, could run things too much his own way. That is why the whole system is based on the idea of checks and balances. That is also the chief reason for having both a Senate and a House of Representatives. Each acts as a "check" to the other; each helps balance the power given by the country.

What every American should always remember is not the long list of facts about what was voted at the Constitutional Convention, but the basic principle of checks and balances that has made the government work. It has some disadvantages. It slows things up. It is apt to cause a tremendous amount of arguing and discussion. But discussion in government is a good thing. In the long run this principle is what has kept any one person, or any one set of people, from bossing the rest of the citizens around too much. The people's votes on Election Day are the final decisive "check."

This system is the reason why the delegates to the Constitutional Convention had to work so hard. It wasn't enough to believe that a system of checks and balances was the right one. They had to devise rules that would make the principle apply in every single instance. Every sentence they wrote had to be closely studied, not only by itself but compared with other items already agreed upon. Who must do what? And where must he stop? It all had to be thought out, so that someone would handle each one of the many, many pieces of business that all together make up good government. And yet there must be no chance left for one officer to say to another, "You keep out of this. This is my business."

It was an enormous relief when, toward the end of that hot July, the convention voted to take a recess. This was the very first break in their every-single-day, all-day-long work since they had arrived in Philadelphia. The recess was to last for ten days, while a special committee studied and considered in even greater detail every word of that Constitution. They were to make sure that no part of it contradicted any other part, and that every sentence of it would stand up in law courts when—perhaps in the future—clever lawyers might try to make a sentence mean what the men who wrote it didn't intend it to mean.

14

Three Old Soldiers

Our Delegate was ready for a rest. But at first he didn't know how he wanted to spend his unexpected vacation. Then he had an idea.

When Debby's father heard what the idea was, and that he was a part of it, he joyfully smacked one hand into the other. Yes, indeed, he would go with the delegate! What's more, he would provide transportation. His son, the farmer, had a steady old horse and a small chaise, just big enough for two, and he would be glad to let them use it for a couple of days.

To Debby's mother he explained, "We think we'd like to make a visit to Valley Forge." He needed to say no more. His wife's face softened as she said thoughtfully, "I'm glad you're going back there. I hear it's all grown over with green things, bushes and grass, so a person, to look at it, would never know the misery of that winter's camp."

"Nature's memory is short—like men's," said her husband.

"I'm glad you have somebody to go with, too," she said. "A fellow soldier who'll know how you are feeling. He won't get upset as I would. I never want to look at that place, knowing what you endured there."

The chaise and the stout old farm horse stood at the door. Debby and her mother trotted to and fro with extra wraps and stockings, and the big lunch basket, and some towels in case the country inn shouldn't be really clean, and a pillow—

"There, there," said Our Delegate, laughing. "We're not going to drive to Georgia. Only to Valley Forge. We'll be back by tomorrow evening. Even if it should rain!"

He helped Debby's father in, settled his crutches beside him, climbed in on the other side, took off his cocked hat and waved it to Debby and her mother. Then he picked up the reins, clucked to the horse, and the chaise jogged away down the street.

"How cheerful they both looked," thought Debby wonderingly. How could two people who had been through such terrible things look like two boys going off fishing together?

It was dusk the next day when the chaise jogged back. The weather had been fair. No rain. Probably everything had gone all right. The two men looked happy.

"We found it had all gone back to a state of Nature," the delegate said, "grass growing thickly where our tents had stood, young trees starting up where the earthworks had been. It made us feel very sober to stand there and look back. And remember.

"We found a place to eat lunch. A corner of what had been the drill ground. An old tree had fallen across it, to make a bench and a table. We sat there, opening your lunch basket, when we saw someone walking down the drill ground toward where we were. We were not surprised. We thought probably some other old soldier had had the same idea we had—to go back and see how it looked. We sat there on the fallen tree, your open lunch basket between us, watching him come across the drill ground. We said to each other that if it did turn out to be a man who had served there as a soldier, we'd invite him to share our meal.

"But as he came across, there was something about the way he walked, the way he carried his head—He was a tall gentleman—" The delegate's breath gave out. He could not say another word.

Debby's father said solemnly, "It was General George Washington."

There was a silence. The two men looked at each other.

"Well," the delegate finally continued, "he ate lunch with us, General George Washington did. He said he had gone back, just the way we did, to look at the place where, that winter—"

He paused. Debby's father said, "We talked things over together, the three of us."

"Oh, how did he look? What did he say?" Debby burst out.

"He looked just as he always does," her father answered quietly. "You know how he looks."

There was a pause. Then he went on. "He didn't say much. He never does," her father added, so softly that he seemed to be almost whispering.

The two men smiled at each other.

And that was all that Debby and her mother ever heard about it.

15

"We Did the Best We Could"

After the vacation, all the delegates—all except the Committee on Detail, which had been on duty steadily without a single day off—came back fresh and ready for more work. It took six weeks more of the same sort of drudgery—rewriting some rule that had looked all right when it was voted, but on second thought didn't seem quite fair to everyone; changing words here and there to make their meaning clear beyond mistake. The work was tiresome. How they longed to go home! They didn't even have the excitement of a hot debate to carry them along—except once. And that was too serious to be amusing. When that dispute broke out, there were a few days when they began to think that all their work had come to nothing. It looked as though they would break up, finally, and go back home, defeated.

None of them had guessed how much dynamite there was in the question of slavery—enough to almost wreck the Union seventy years later! In the earliest days of the new nation, slaves had been kept in all the colonies. There were never many in the North, where they did not fit into the way farms were run. But there were more and more of them as you went south. By the time of the convention in 1787, Massachusetts had forbidden slavery and eight States allowed no new slaves to be brought inside their borders. Almost everywhere, in Virginia as well as in New Hampshire, forward-looking leaders thought it a great pity that the system had ever been started. They hoped it would die out. None of these leaders—at least none who were in the Constitutional Convention—were willing to go so far as to make laws to free the slaves already in America. Governor Randolph expressed what most of them thought, when he said he was sorry such a special property (slaves) existed. But since it did exist, he supposed the right to it would have to be protected by the law, like any other property.

But bringing in new slaves from Africa in slave ships was something else. It was well known that they suffered frightfully during the voyage. Nearly everybody thought that was wrong. They wanted it to stop. And the lid blew off in the hottest quarrel of the convention when South Carolina insisted that it be written into the Constitution that Congress should never stop the slave trade.

All the debates about this were angry. In one of the most furious ones, Mr. Martin of Maryland called slavery the right to import more new slaves from Africa. But not forever, just for twenty years more. New England was given (as the price of their votes) a freer chance to make laws about shipping. No one was very proud or satisfied about this bargain, but at least, once more, the convention had been kept from going to pieces.

The next two weeks went quickly. Whole sections of the Constitution were voted with scarcely any debate. It was almost as if everyone was anxious not to start any more trouble. Finally, about the middle of September, their work was finished. Actually all finished. They could hardly believe it.

The last word had been written. But still their troubles were not over. One last action was needed—the signing of the document. Many of the delegates were angry about sections of the Constitution that they didn't like and had worked hard to cut out. Not one of them had had his own way entirely in the convention. Some of them were so bitter about the times when they had been voted down that it was feared they might not be willing to set their names to the great paper. And if a lot of the delegates who had actually been at the convention didn't sign it because they didn't like parts of it, there wouldn't be much chance of getting it accepted out in the different States.

On Monday, the 17th of September, they came together for the last time in the hall where they had worked so long and so hard—since the 25th of May. They were very worried. Nobody knew yet how many of the members would refuse to sign. Could it be that at the very end the convention would fail?

The secretary read the Constitution aloud in its final form. When he had finished, old Dr. Franklin immediately heaved himself up on his tottery legs and started to speak. But it hurt him too much to stand. He sank back into his chair while Mr. Wilson took the written speech and read it aloud.

Like all Benjamin Franklin's speeches, there was no slam-bang hurrah about it. At first it sounded very ordinary. Then, gradually, everyone began to see that as usual what Franklin said was full of good sense. He made the problem before them seem clear and simple. "Many a time in my life," it ran, "I have been absolutely sure I was right—only to change my mind a year or two later. Some people never change their minds. They are always rather ridiculous. I once knew a lady who told me that her sister said to her, 'It's the strangest thing. Whenever I get into a dispute with somebody, *I've* always been the one who was right.'"

Here he waited a moment for the laugh from the delegates which they couldn't keep back, angry and anxious though they were. He went on, "Now, to tell the truth, there are several points I do not greatly like about this Constitution. That is, I do not like them now. But if I can judge from the past, it is quite likely that I will like them next year. And I am sure of this: that the combined wisdom of so many thoughtful men is certain to be sounder as a whole than anything any one of us could have written alone. So I hope each of you will join me in forgetting the little you dislike here and there in it, and show your approval of the whole effort—and really it is far better than we had any right to hope for—by signing it now, and later supporting it before the people."

Then Alexander Hamilton jumped up. "Everybody knows how different this Constitution is from the one *I* favored." All along he had been for cutting States' rights down to almost nothing. "But the choice, as I see it, is between no government at all—for that is what we have now—and a government that may very well turn out to be better than we now expect. I certainly shall sign."

Three delegates held back—Mason, Randolph, and Gerry—but they were not enough to prevent the Constitution from being the unanimous choice of all the States represented at the convention.

There was no cheering. It was over. They had lived through it. The Constitution had been written. It was approved and passed by vote. It was signed.

Now they could go home at last! The meeting adjourned. The delegates ate their last meal together at the City Tavern. They shook hands and said good-bye soberly to one another.

There was no excitement at Debby's home either. It was not a bit like the day when they had heard the Declaration read. Their delegate came home carrying a package which, somewhat embarrassed, he gave to Debby's mother. It was a clock—a handsome clock for their living room mantel. They never before had seen such a small, dainty clock.

Then he excused himself. He must put his papers in order and pack his valise. He had secured a place on an early coach the very next day. He knew they would understand his leaving at once. It had been a long time since he had seen his family. He went up to his room.

In the morning after breakfast, he thanked them for their hospitality. They wished him good luck. To Debby's father he said, "I'll never, as long as I live, forget our lunch at Valley Forge." The two men shook hands on that memory.

The Philadelphia family stood by the door to watch him walk down the street toward the place where the coach was to start. Halfway to the corner, he turned and came back to them. "I can't leave you good friends without saying—" He hesitated, set down his valise bulging with his extra shirts, rubbed his chin, went on. "I feel I ought to tell you that we know we made mistakes. Sometimes, I fear, we did wrong." He went on so sadly that their spirits were darkened. "There come times when it does not seem possible to do what is really right. The choice seems to be between doing what is not good and—something that would be worse. But we did the best we could."

Now he turned to Debby, and his voice was brighter. "You, my dear child—all you younger people—our trust is in you. We have provided in the Constitution for amendments—ways to correct the mistakes we did not know enough to avoid. Never forget that the Constitution can be amended. The best people of our nation will always, generation after generation, keep trying to improve it. We who have worked so hard on it will go down to our graves trusting that the Americans of the future will love freedom and justice as we have—and serve them better."

He took Debby's hand in his. "May you and your children and your grandchildren—and mine—always be on the side of those who are working for more justice and more freedom." He said this so earnestly that it sounded almost like a prayer.

Then he put on his hat, bowed to them all, and went away. They never saw him again.

But they did hear from him. Next July came a polite letter asking about their health and then, fairly boiling over with pride, "I have heard that New Hampshire has ratified the Constitution, and almost at the same time, Virginia. That makes ten States accepting our Constitution. Now the government of the United States of America will be formed without delay."

The spring after that came a shorter note to Debby's father, beginning, "Dear Comrade:—With what joy we both learn that our former Commander in Chief is now President Washington!"

A year and a half later, near Christmas time, he wrote in joyful relief, "One of my greatest regrets is gone. One of our greatest mistakes is corrected. The Amendments for the Bill of Rights are now part of the Constitution.

16

What You Might Call a Postscript

Fifty-three years after Debby and her family had said good-bye to their delegate and watched him walk away from them down the street, the United States government published the notes taken down in shorthand by Mr. Madison on the proceedings of the Constitutional Convention in 1787. It was the first chance anybody had ever had to know, completely, what had gone on in that big hall in Philadelphia where the fate of the nation had been decided.

Debby and her husband sent at once to Washington to buy the three big volumes. They cost a good deal. The price was more than they would ordinarily have thought of spending on a book. But like other Americans of their age, they had wondered for fifty years about the details of that convention.

A few of the delegates as they grew older had talked about it. Some of the discussion had been set down. But these odds and ends of notes and memories contradicted each other so completely that not much could be learned from them.

Now the whole official record had been printed. Now anybody could find out what had been kept so secret all those years.

When the big package came in from Washington, Debby was alone in the house. Her husband was down at the bank. They had planned to go through the books together. But Debby couldn't wait to begin. There was one meeting of that long-ago convention she was especially curious about. *Why* did the delegate who roomed with her family in Philadelphia seem so low-spirited all through the first part of July, and then suddenly one day come home smiling, with a bouquet of roses for her birthday, and say that evening that Mr. Wilson of Pennsylvania was "an honor to the human race"? She remembered the exact date. It was her birthday, July 13th.

She opened the package of books, looked through them to see which one of the three was for July, put on her steel-rimmed reading spectacles, sat down in her favorite rocking chair, and turned to July 13th.

Suddenly her eye was caught by a phrase—"moved to strike out the word 'wealth.' " And here was Mr. Wilson's speech, here was the reason her delegate had looked so happy after having been so sad. "All men, wherever placed, have equal rights," Mr. Wilson began. ". . . If the new western States ever have more voters, we should not, we cannot deny them their fair share of representation in Congress. . . . And finally, as for the argument of my opponents, I disagree absolutely. Property is *not* the sole or primary object of government and society. The most noble object of government is the cultivation and improvement of the human mind." A feeling of great pride overwhelmed her. Mr. Wilson had spoken for America at its best. And the delegates had acted like the best kind of Americans. Every single State but one had voted to strike out the word "wealth." No wonder their delegate was proud and happy the evening of her birthday.

So that settled it. No, as she turned over the page she came on another effort to keep lawmaking power in the settled East. Though wealth was now given up as a measuring rod, some of the delegates had suggested writing into the Constitution a fixed rule that no new State could ever outvote the old thirteen.

Again someone had spoken for America as it was to be. This time with the voice of old Mr. Sherman, who had started life as a shoemaker, taught himself, and later represented his State. "We are providing for our children and grandchildren," he said, "and they are as likely to be citizens of the new States as of the old ones. I am against any restrictions." Again the best spirit of America had come to life with his generous words. The vote of the convention sustained him. No restrictions were voted.

What did that vote mean? Debby asked herself. And

she thought joyfully, "Why, it meant free and equal government for all the States where my children now live—Ohio, Michigan, Indiana, Illinois. She counted on her fingers. Yes, there were thirteen new States since the Constitution had been adopted, just double the old number, far more than double the size. To say nothing of—maybe, who knew?—more to come on the other side of the Mississippi.

What would have happened if those delegates had not stuck at it until they had put together a set of rules that could be stretched to take in all that new country? And how fascinating it was to look at last behind those closed doors!

She turned over page after page, not reading steadily—that would come on long winter evenings—but stopping only when some striking event caught her eye. How did it end? She opened the last volume. Why, late, late—even at the end of August it had still been uncertain. Mr. Martin had been sure the people would never accept the Constitution if they took time to think it over. Mr. Gerry agreed. The system proposed, he thought, was full of vices. Mr. Mason said he would sooner chop off his right hand than sign the Constitution as it stood then. And Mr. Morris snapped back at them, "All right, let's go home and leave everything to another convention that will have the courage to provide a vigorous government, which *we are afraid to do.*"

But they had not given up. They stayed, and as her delegate had said, they did the best they could. She understood now why he had been so solemn when he had said good-bye. After those months of strain, none of them could be sure that their work had any value. Her heart melted. She hoped her delegate had lived long enough to hear the men at the convention spoken of as the "Founding Fathers." Everyone called them that now. And they deserved it. In those long, long days of debate and deep thought, they had hammered out a system which worked, which had endured, which would endure.

Drawing a long breath of relief, she looked up.

To her surprise four of her grandchildren stood there, rosy and smiling, their coats and caps still on, their skates hanging on their shoulders. Debby's ears as well as her eyes were now rather dulled by age. She had not heard them come into the house, as they often did after school or play.

"We just clumped up the stairs," they said, "but you were so deep in your reading you never heard a sound. We've been standing here watching you. That must be an exciting story."

One of them leaned over her shoulder and read out the title:

DEBATES OF THE CONSTITUTIONAL
CONVENTION IN 1787
as set down by Mr. James Madison

The youngsters broke into groans. "Oh, Granny, how *can* you read such a dull book?"

At this, to their great surprise, their grandmother broke into a merry, ringing laugh.

What could be the joke?

She pulled off her reading spectacles to see them more clearly. Her eyes were still crinkled at the corners from her laugh. "Dull!" she said, and laughed again. "It's the most exciting book I ever read in all my life! And to think I lived through all of it and never really knew what was going on!"

suit of Happiness.—That to secure these rights, Governments are instituted among Men, deriving their just powers from the consent of the governed,—That whenever any Form of Government becomes destructive of these ends, it is the Right of the People to alter or to abolish it, and to institute a new Government, laying its foundation on such principles and organizing its powers in such form, as to them shall seem most likely to effect their Safety and Happiness. Prudence, indeed, will dictate that Governments long established should not be changed for light and transient causes; and accordingly all experience hath shewn, that mankind are more disposed to suffer, while evils are sufferable, than to right themselves by abolishing the forms to which they are accustomed. But when a long train of abuses and usurpations, pursuing invariably the same Object evinces a design to reduce them under absolute Despotism, it is their right, it is their duty, to throw off such Government, and to provide new Guards for their future security.— Such has been the patient sufferance of these Colonies; and such is now the necessity which constrains them to alter their former Systems of Government.The history of the present King of Great Britain is a history of repeated injuries and usurpations, all having in direct object the establishment of an absolute Tyranny over these States. To prove this, let Facts be submitted to a candid world.— He has refused his Assent to Laws, the most wholesome and necessary for the public good.—He has forbidden his Governors to pass Laws of immediate and pressing importance, unless suspended in their operation till his Assent should be obtained; and when so suspended, he has utterly neglected to attend to them.—He has refused to pass other Laws for the accommodation of large districts of people, unless those people would relinquish the right of Representation in the Legislature, a right inestimable to them and formidable to tyrants only.—He has called together legislative bodies at places unusual, uncomfortable, and distant from the depository of their public Records, for the sole purpose of fatiguing them into compliance with his measures.—He has dissolved Representative Houses repeatedly, for opposing with manly firmness his invasions on the rights of the people.—He has refused for a long time, after such dissolutions, to cause others to be elected; whereby the Legislative Powers, incapable of Annihilation, have returned to the People at large for their exercise; the State remaining in the mean time exposed to all the dangers of invasion from without, and convulsions within.—He has endeavoured to prevent the population of these States; for that purpose obstructing the Laws for Naturalization of Foreigners; refusing to pass others to encourage their migrations hither, and raising the conditions of new Appropriations of Lands.—He has obstructed the Administration of Justice, by refusing his Assent to Laws for establishing Judiciary Powers.—He has made Judges dependent on his Will alone, for the tenure of their offices, and the amount and payment of their salaries. He has erected a multitude of New Offices, and sent hither swarms of Officers to harass our people, and eat out their substance.—He has kept among us, in times of peace, Standing Armies without the Consent of our legislatures.—He has affected to render the Military independent of and superior to the Civil Power.—He has combined with others to subject us to a jurisdiction foreign to our constitution, and unacknowledged by our laws; giving his Assent to their Acts of pretended Legislation:—For quartering large bodies of armed troops among us:—For protecting them, by a mock Trial, from punishment for any Murders which they should commit on the Inhabitants of these States:—For cutting off our Trade with all parts of the world:—For imposing Taxes on us without our Consent:—For depriving us in many cases, of the benefits of Trial by Jury:—For transporting us beyond Seas to be tried for pretended offences:—For abolishing the free System of English Laws in a neighbouring Province, establishing therein an Arbitrary government, and enlarging its Boundaries so as to render it at once an example and fit instrument for introducing the same absolute rule into these Colonies:—For taking away our Charters, abolishing our most valuable Laws and altering fundamentally the Forms of our Governments:—For suspending our own Legislatures, and declaring themselves invested with power to legislate for us in all cases whatsoever.—He has abdicated Government here, by declaring us out of his Protection and waging War against us.—He has plundered our seas, ravaged our Coasts, burnt our towns, and destroyed the lives of our people.—He is at this time transporting large Armies of foreign Mercenaries to compleat the works of death, desolation and tyranny, already begun with circumstances of Cruelty & perfidy scarcely paralleled in the most barbarous ages, and totally unworthy the Head of a civilized nation.—He has constrained our fellow Citizens taken Captive on the high Seas to bear Arms against their Country, to become the executioners of their friends and Brethren, or to fall themselves by their Hands.—He has excited domestic insurrections amongst us, and has endeavoured to bring on the inhabitants of our frontiers, the merciless Indian Savages, whose known rule of warfare, is an undistinguished destruction of all ages, sexes and conditions. In every stage of these Oppressions We have Petitioned for Redress in the most humble terms: Our repeated Petitions have been answered only by repeated injury. A Prince, whose character is thus marked by every act which may define a Tyrant, is unfit to be the ruler of a free people. Nor have We been wanting in attentions to our British brethren. We have warned them, from time to time, of attempts by their legislature to extend an unwarrantable jurisdiction over us. We have reminded them of the circumstances of our emigration and settlement here. We have appealed to their native justice and magnanimity, and we have conjured them by the ties of our common kindred to disavow these usurpations, which would inevitably interrupt our connections and correspondence. They too have been deaf to the voice of justice and of consanguinity. We must,

John Penn

Edward Rutledge

Thos. Heyward, Jr.

Thomas Lynch, Jr.

Arthur Middleton

Samuel Chase

Wm. Paca

Thos. Stone

Charles Carroll of
  Carrollton

George Wythe

Richard Henry Lee

Th. Jefferson

Benj. Harrison

Benj. Franklin

John Morton

Geo. Clymer

Jas. Smith

Geo. Taylor

James Wilson

Geo. Ross

Caesar Rodney

Geo. Read

Tho. M:Kean

Wm. Floyd

Phil. Livingston

Frans. Lewis

Josiah Bartlett

Wm. Whipple

Saml. Adams

John Adams

Robt. Treat Paine

Elbridge Gerry

Step. Hopkins

William Ellery

Roger Sherman

Sam. Huntington

Wm. Williams

Oliver Wolcott

Matthew Thornton